# Jealousy Self-Help

*How to Overcome Jealousy and Possessiveness in Relationships to STOP Being Insecure and why it happens.*

*The Cure to Not Be Jealous Is Already Within You. Learn to Trust and Save Your Relationship!*

© **Copyright 2019 - All rights reserved.**

The content contained within this book may not be reproduced, duplicated or transmitted without direct written permission from the author or the publisher.

Under no circumstances will any blame or legal responsibility be held against the publisher, or author, for any damages, reparation, or monetary loss due to the information contained within this book. Either directly or indirectly.

Legal Notice:

This book is copyright protected. This book is only for personal use. You cannot amend, distribute, sell, use, quote or paraphrase any part, or the content within this book, without the consent of the author or publisher.

Disclaimer Notice:

Please note the information contained within this document is for educational and entertainment purposes only. All effort has been executed to present accurate, up to date, and reliable, complete information. No warranties of any kind are declared or implied. Readers acknowledge that the author is not engaging in the rendering of legal, financial, medical or professional advice. The content within this book has been derived from various sources. Please consult a licensed professional before attempting any techniques outlined in this book.

By reading this document, the reader agrees that under no circumstances is the author responsible for any losses, direct or indirect, which are incurred as a result of the use of information contained within this document, including, but not limited to, — errors, omissions, or inaccuracies.

# Table of Contents

*Introduction* ............................................................ 1

*Chapter 1: Theoretical Concept of Jealousy* .. 3

   Scientific View ............................................... 3

   Sociological View ........................................... 5

   Psychological View ......................................... 6

   Jealousy and Envy ......................................... 7

*Chapter 2: What Type of Jealousy Are You Feeling?* ............................................................... 9

   Romantic Jealousy ......................................... 9

   Abnormal Jealousy ...................................... 11

   Sexual Jealousy ........................................... 12

   Is There Positive and Negative Jealousy? .. 13

   Is Jealousy Gender-Based? ........................ 16

*Chapter 3: Why Are You Jealous?* ............... 18

   Biological Evolution ................................... 18

   Jealousy after Betrayal .............................. 19

Inferiority Complex ................................... 21

Myths, Assumptions, and Generalization . 24

Expectations .............................................. 26

Investment in the Relationship.................. 29

Aging ........................................................... 30

*Chapter 4: How Jealousy Hurts You .......... 33*

*Chapter 5: Why Jealousy Drives Your Partner Away ..............................................40*

*Chapter 6: How to Track and Control Your Emotions......................................................46*

Stop Being a Perfectionist..........................50

Perform a Personality Test to Understand Yourself Better ........................................... 52

Keep a Journal to Track Your Emotions ... 54

Improve Your Emotional Intelligence ...... 56

Concentrate on the Things That Matter .... 59

Overcome Jealousy after Betrayal ............ 61

Overcome Your Inferiority Complex......... 64

Do Not Jump to Conclusions......................66

Understanding That No One Is Perfect .....69

*Chapter 7: Custom-Fit Approach to Jealousy for Different Couples........................................ 71*

Understand Your Partner's Love Language ................................................................73

Communicative Responses .......................76

Understanding Each Other's Philosophy of Love and a Healthy Relationship ............. 80

Overcoming Assumptions .........................82

Escaping the Threat of Communication Technologies and Social Media ................. 86

Working as a Team ................................... 88

*Chapter 8: How to Identify Triggers of Jealousy......................................................95*

*Chapter 9: How to Mentally Step Back from Jealous Reactions ....................................... 107*

Becoming Aware .........................................108

Recovering Personal Power ...................... 110

Shifting Your Point of View ..................... 111

Knowing the Beliefs and Values within You That Trigger Emotional Reactions ........... 112

The Other Approach Is Developing Control over Your Attention ...................................114

Talk about the Feeling of Jealousy ........... 115

Train Your Mind to Be Competitive, Appreciative, Encouraging, and Acknowledging ......................................... 117

## Chapter 10: Gentle Approaches of Acceptance ................................................................119

Jealousy Can Strike Anyone.................... 120

Jealousy Should Not Be the Reason You Part with Your Partner..................................... 122

You Should Not Let Jealousy Control You: Why Not Control Your Imagination? ...... 123

You Can Make It: You Can Feel Jealous but Control It ................................................. 124

How about You Stop Making Unreasonable

Comparisons? ............................................. 125

Nothing Is Permanent ............................ 126

*Do Not Hold Too Tight* ............................. 128

**Chapter 11: Exercises for Making Yourself Better** ....................................................... 130

    Compete Only against Yourself ............... 130

    Develop the Mind of a Winner ................. 131

    Develop Daily Good Habits ...................... 133

    Eat Healthy, Dress Smart, and Exercise .. 134

    Meditate .................................................... 135

    Build Confidence ...................................... 137

    Celebrate Small Successes ...................... 139

    Declutter Your Life ................................... 140

**Chapter 12: Loving Yourself Unconditionally** ..................................................................... 142

**Chapter 13: How to Deal with Another Person's Jealousy toward You** .................. 150

**Chapter 14: Real-Life Examples of Jealousy**

*Cases and Solutions* .................................... *163*

  *A Case of Jealousy after Betrayal* ............ *163*

  *A Case of Inferiority Complex* .................. *164*

  *A Case of Assumptions* ............................ *165*

  *A Case of Expectations* ........................... *166*

  *A Case of Investment in the Relationship* *167*

  *A Case of Aging* ........................................ *168*

*Chapter 15: Recap: Summary of Lessons Learned and How to Maintain a Healthy Relationship* ............................................. *170*

*Conclusion* .................................................. *178*

*Bibliography* .............................................. *182*

# Introduction

In its simplest definition, jealousy is the thought or feeling of fear and insecurity. It is a result of the threats to self-esteem and the fear of loss. Jealousy is everywhere—in workplaces, in learning institutions, and even in family settings. Relationships are not an exception. The bitter truth is that jealousy threatens even the strongest human bond. Most often, the problem is not the jealous feelings that we have; it is how you respond to the feelings that matter.

Everyone is jealous at some point in their relationships. It is hard to pinpoint an individual who has never felt jealous. Think about it. It is almost impossible to go about your entire relationship without having a tingle of envy or some passionate suspicion. Sometimes the feeling is intense, but other times, it is slight or mild. However, jealousy can easily take over our relationships, our joy, and our peace. It can make us angry, depressed, and agitated. It can take over our emotions.

Since jealousy is destructive, we have to know why we feel jealous. We need to realize why we are most often the cause of our sufferings. This book gives you a closer look at jealousy and shows you why and how you don't have to bring your own sufferings in your relationship. Certainly, you don't want to suffer. It doesn't make sense to be controlled by your jealous feelings and thereby bring suffering to you and your partner.

# Chapter 1: Theoretical Concept of Jealousy

For a long time, psychologists, sociologists, and scientists have strived to dissect the concept of jealousy in their attempt to understand its causes and cure, as evidenced by research (Kristjánsson, 2016). Normally, jealousy consists of one or more emotions, including inadequacy, bitterness, fury, and repulsion. Jealousy manifests either as reactive or suspicious, and there are various factors that lead to it. Sociologists have argued that different people have different ways of expressing jealousy, mainly based on the cultural or social setup they grow up in. Also, scientists have discovered that there are factors that may reflexively stimulate someone to express jealousy.

## Scientific View

Since jealousy is manifested in various types of behaviors and reactions, scientists have not had a consensus on a single definition. Instead, various definitions are put across, but they share common themes. From one scientific perspective, jealousy entails a complex set of feelings, thoughts, and actions as a result of esteem issues. It is detrimental to a relationship. Most of the time, the jealous partner perceives a potential attraction between their partner and a potential rival.

Moreover, jealousy is usually a person's reaction when the partner is showing unacceptable behaviors in the relationship. This is one of the most dreaded occurrences when one is in a relationship. Hence, thoughts and reactions toward such likelihood come off as jealousy. Furthermore, jealousy can be seen as an expressive, rational, and behavioral retort to a threat in a relationship. This definition reflects the various types of jealousy.

For instance, a sexually jealous partner is likely to show an emotional or behavioral response to the suspicion that their partner is sexually attracted to or desires to engage in sexual activity with another person. One can also show these reactions if their partner seems to have an emotional involvement with another person. Additionally, jealousy is defined as a defensive response to the perception of a threat in a relationship in which a partner's conduct seems to be contrary to the other person's meaning of their relationship. Finally, scientists define jealousy as a phenomenon that is triggered by the threat of loss or separation from a partner whenever there seems to be some interest with a third party.

All these definitions portray jealousy as a phenomenon that occurs when there is a perceived third party. Jealousy involves emotional reactions perceived as conscious and unconscious efforts to try protecting a relationship, and jealousy comes as a result of a threat.

## Sociological View

Sociology views jealousy as an aspect that varies across cultures and whose expression within a cultural setup changes over time. It is argued that, as a result of increased civilization and freedom in the contemporary setup, people are increasingly able to express their jealous feelings. Also, there is much to be jealous about since people have more options and various cultures encourage maximum interaction and socialization. Furthermore, the rise of communication technologies encourages people to interact with various people at the same time.

## Psychological View

Psychology portrays jealousy as a complex emotional phenomenon that most often originates from perceptions, thoughts, and feelings of déjà vu; and a jealous person's reaction is most often emotional (Ellis & Weinstein, 1986). Jealousy is said to have a social or cultural origin. Society matters a lot in the development of such a feeling.

From a psychological perspective, jealousy has been paramount in the evolution of our genes. It has been used to endorse the paternity of a person's young one. For instance, jealousy in men is often a result of not wanting to waste their time, efforts, and resources in taking care of another person's young one, as well as not wanting to be sexually betrayed. However, the pattern of reasoning in this manner is highly influenced by cultural orientation. In fact, jealousy is considered as an emotion that occurs from the result of an individual's needs not being met. In psychology, it is largely linked to low self-esteem and aggression. Also, it is known to increase a person's passion for their partners.

## Jealousy and Envy

Although the two have become synonymous, jealousy is different from envy in its original meaning. In some instances, the terms are used indiscriminately, such as jealousy being composed of passions (e.g., lust, greed, and envy). There appears a blurred line between the uses of the two very close yet very different terms. Perhaps, this coinciding use and understanding of these terms happen because individuals can experience both phenomena at the same time. For instance, if a person envies the characteristics possessed by a perceived rival, they become jealous in the relationship, maybe jealous that their partner may be giving the perceived rival some level of attention that according to them belongs to them only. Thus, in modern society, people perceive jealousy as a label that stands for both terms.

However, jealousy and envy are differentiated by the exact thought or emotion that one experiences. While a jealous person is full of thoughts of how to keep something that one has, an envious person desires to have what others have that they do not. An envious person has feelings of longing, motivation to improve, desire to possess the qualities of a rival, and even inferiority. A jealous person, on the other hand, is full of fear of loss, mistrust, doubtfulness, sadness over imagined loss, and suspicion of betrayal. Nevertheless, envy is a major cause for jealousy; hence, the two situations can be experienced concurrently. Being envious intensify jealous emotions.

# Chapter 2: What Type of Jealousy Are You Feeling?

Jealousy remains one of the most destructive forces in human existence. It has been associated with the most number of relationship breakups, as well as murders and suicides. Jealous people go to the extent of harming their partners when the partner seem unstoppable in their attraction to a third party. Others harm themselves because their self-esteem lowers when they identify that another person is making their partner happier to the extent that they deem themselves worthless. There are various types of jealousy that people exhibit.

**Romantic Jealousy**

Romantic jealousy is the most popular type of jealousy in relationships today. It arises from the point of romantic interest. It is a complex feeling that results from a threat to the quality of the relationship when a romantic interest between one's partner and a third party (perhaps a rival) is perceived. This threat is posed to the self and the relationship. One develops thoughts of insecurity that the chemistry in the relationship is fading away as another party progressively takes their place. One is threatened by emotional infidelity.

Most people who have shown interest in another person while still in a committed relationship have argued that their feelings faded away in the relationship they were in. The knowledge that it is almost impossible to stop a heart-to-heart attraction is what sparks jealousy when a partner seems to have romantic tendencies with a perceived or perhaps potential rival. When you are romantically jealous, you are perhaps afraid to admit that there may not be enough romantic feelings necessary for a relationship to thrive, and you may be too afraid to lose your partner to someone else who is currently able to fulfill their romantic feelings.

## Abnormal Jealousy

This type of jealousy is perhaps the most destructive form of jealousy. It can also be described by words such as "morbid," "delusional," and "psychotic." Usually, highly immature and insecure people will experience this kind of jealousy. Some people want to be in control when they get into a relationship. They cannot take it when a perceived rival seems to have some form of contact with their partner. Such immaturity and desire to be in control often lead to irrational thoughts and actions under which a relationship cannot thrive.

If you are experiencing this kind of jealousy, you want to know every single thing that your partner is doing. You want to know everyone they are talking to and to monitor each of their moves. In the world today, where the internet and the communication technologies are paramount, you may want to track down the GPS location of your partner. Some people even go to the extent of tapping their partner's communications, such as messages and calls, without their knowledge. Applications have been designed to run in the background of other people's communication devices and project all information to the interested party, who in this case is an extremely jealous person.

**Sexual Jealousy**

This kind of jealousy occurs from the feelings and thoughts that your partner may be having or intends to engage in some sexual relations with a third party. It is often triggered by the uncertainty that the relationship would continue to thrive peacefully after your partner engages in sexual relations with a rival. Also, if you are experiencing this kind of jealousy, perhaps you are uncomfortable with the thought of sharing your partner with another person sexually. You definitely believe that everything in the relationship should be exclusively shared between the two of you. You experience a trigger when your partner shows some sexual interest in another person. Most often, people engage in sexual infidelity and hide this from their partners to protect their relationship. Scientists believe that sexual jealousy is part of biological processes as partners attempt to identify the most sexually compatible partners.

## Is There Positive and Negative Jealousy?

There are various types of jealousy, but the most contentious issue is if there is positive and negative jealousy. There are various examples of jealousy in different cultures. Most of them are associated with negativity. Jealous emotions impose in you the fear of losing your partner and being betrayed by a supposed narcissist. Obviously, this is not a pleasant feeling, especially when you have experienced betrayal in the past.

However, it is always important to look at both sides of everything, hence to examine if jealousy has a positive side. I believe that there is some positive aspect of jealousy, and that is when it serves a warning. There are people out there who are just malicious, and their personality leads them to think that they can get anything they want and at any time.

Therefore, they may want to prove this by snatching away someone who is in a committed relationship. Therefore, in such instances, if one notices some strange interactions between such a person and their partner, they become positively jealous because they stand up to defend their territories.

Anyone can lose their partner because of recklessness. Being jealous can be positive energy to motivate you to work toward preventing this loss. If anything, having someone that others admire means you are fortunate and on the right track. This does not make you a victim of some sort or make the admirers the bad guys. It only shows that your partner has something valuable that triggers envy. In such a situation, jealousy reflects an approach of cautiousness about that which you deem yours. And it is positive since it calls upon you to defend something that belongs to you.

Furthermore, jealousy is considered positive when one is boasting about their well-being while you are undergoing a rough time in life. This reflects the nature of immaturity or people who are dealing with low self-esteem themselves, and they need to boast just to make themselves feel better. Even if it is a case of immaturity on the person who is boasting, it does not make it any less irritating, and this might make you jealous. If a person directly attacks you on the basis of something that they have and you don't have, you can't help but respond with a jealous attitude toward that thing that you feel offensive. However irritating and immature this is, take it as a rule of thumb not to pay attention to such things. It is just not worth your thoughts and time.

Also, when you are intentionally ignored, jealousy tends to creep in. When your partner does not acknowledge your feelings, achievements, or good deeds, yet at the same time, they happen to mention how attractive or thoughtful another person is, it is natural to become jealous. Naturally, everyone expects their partner to be their biggest cheerer. Everyone wants to come first in their partner's life. They want to be acknowledged, or maybe they want to be challenged to improve. Jealousy arises when you feel undervalued and think you are not given the position you think you deserve in your partner's life.

However, as real as these instances of positive jealousy are, bowing down to them is what transforms into negative jealousy. There is a very fine line between negative and positive jealousy. As mentioned earlier, it is innate in us to feel envious at times. It becomes negative jealousy when you allow the jealousy feelings to grow unremittingly. The feelings overwhelm you, and they determine your behavior. Essentially, it is how you manage your envious feeling that determines whether you have negative or positive jealousy.

**Is Jealousy Gender-Based?**

There are different forms of jealousy for different genders. The major reason for this could be that men and women view dating and relationships differently. Both genders possess different perceptions about sexual relations, dating, committed relationships, and attachment. Women tend to fear emotional infidelity more than sexual infidelity. They fear abandonment; hence, jealousy tends to manifest if they suspect an impending abandonment. Emotional jealousy is perceived to be more responsive in females than in males. Emotionally jealous women are more aggressive and violent than emotionally jealous men.

On the flip side, sexual jealousy tends to manifest more in men than in women. While women are disturbed by signs of withdrawal, men are disturbed by the thought of their partner engaging in sexual relations with another man. This difference between these genders is further amplified by the societal standards. Most of the time, individuals tend to pick up experiences within their family units as they grow up. Different genders internalize what the society has placed as their worth in interpersonal relationships. That being said, both genders are concerned about the different things that are there to be jealous about.

# Chapter 3: Why Are You Jealous?

As destructive as jealousy can be, it is good to understand the various reasons why it occurs. Understanding the root cause for jealousy forms the platform for finding solutions to it. Jealousy is described as an involuntary feeling that has underlying triggers.

The following is a checklist of some reasons why you might be feeling jealous:

**Biological Evolution**

Jealousy is considered to be part of human evolution. All organisms seek to maximize their chances for survival by competing for available yet scarce resources. Thus, jealousy is known to be innate in humans since childhood. The clearest case is that of a first-born who feels unwanted when a second-born child joins the family and the attention of the parents shifts to that child. Children exhibit jealousy in various ways, and parents are normally in a constant struggle trying to balance the love and attention to be equal among all their children. Jealousy then is a competitive emotion that continues into adulthood and exhibits in relationships. You become jealous because you found your partner and you feel entitled to have them. You consider them to be a rare resource that is dear to you, and you are willing to compete for it. Hence, you are jealous if there is any threat that indicates someone else may take away your partner.

**Jealousy after Betrayal**

Betrayal is perhaps the most frustrating feeling one can have in a relationship. To experience betrayal, you must have trusted your partner at first. Then the unexpected happened, and that was a betrayal. In this case, a person that you trusted violated your trust. This could be an ex-lover or the current partner.

Betrayal accounts for most of the insecurity that exists in a relationship. A partner betrays you by having an affair with someone else, for lying to you, and even for hurting you by putting their selfish interests first. Someone's deliberate hurtful actions and carelessness or personal weaknesses hurt a partner because it feels like the choice they made was wrong and preventable in the first place. Even if you forgive a partner who betrayed you, there tends to be a sense of guarding your heart that you develop, and you always stay alert to avoid a repeat of betrayal. Your level of trust lowers, and you tend to notice even the slightest mistakes that your partner has.

Furthermore, your tendencies to be jealous could be because of abandonment. Some people tend to be affected by a loss or betrayal they experienced in their childhood to their relationships in adulthood. For instance, people trace their jealousy to have learned that one of their parents had cheated on the other and no one else knew about it but him. They could not trust another person after going through that situation. Other people were abandoned by their previous lovers, and they were devastated. What matters after such an experience is the process of healing. Some incidences of betrayal leave the greatest of scars in our hearts and make us to never really trust again. Thus, we may get jealous over the slightest cases of provocation.

**Inferiority Complex**

In its simplest form, "inferiority complex" is the subconscious feeling that others are superior to you. This intense feeling develops in a person's life, depending on their upbringing and the instances in which they have been discouraged. A long history of discouragement makes one feel like they are inferior and these feelings are hard to forego. Unfortunately, for most of us, we have had to learn it the hard way that we can do anything that we set our hearts and efforts to. Growing up, we never experienced encouraging words from our parents that could teach us to believe in our abilities. For some of us, even the sociocultural setups we grew up in were hostile, and they led us to think of ourselves as inferior beings.

Discrimination on the basis of gender, race, and religion gets into our heads over time. Facing criticism in various aspects of life can also get into our heads. Also, educational and professional setbacks make us feel like we truly cannot make it in life. Another cause for the inferiority complex is constant comparisons that make us feel uncomfortable in our own skin. In the modern world, where we are able to see other people's achievements in so many ways, it is easy to develop a sense of inferiority and feel like we cannot make it in anything. Physical shortcomings also go a long way in the development of inferiority since we tend to compare ourselves with others and think that we are not attractive enough. When we develop low self-esteem and stick negativity in our brains, it will gradually affect our relationships in a bad way. It places us in an unfavorable position relative to other people.

Now, inferiority complex is a major cause for jealousy since one may always feel like they cannot fully satisfy their partner, yet at the same time, they are so afraid to lose the partner to someone else who seems like they have it better. Because of the performance anxiety that low self-esteem creates, one has a constant need for approval. People with low self-esteem constantly degrade themselves. They are anxious, and they fear failure or being rejected. Feeling inferior can cause you to become possessive because you think that eventually, you are going to be rejected on the basis of who you are. You tend to become jealous over the slightest instance of being provoked. Considering yourself as an underachiever can make you think that your partner is constantly looking for someone who has more achievements. You become envious of other people's achievements, and you get jealous when such people have contact with your partner.

In fact, the inferiority complex leads you to think that you have no options if you parted with the current partner. You are engulfed by the fear of the unknown future if the current relationship does not work. You feel that this relationship is essential for your happiness and that you wouldn't be attractive to another person.

## Myths, Assumptions, and Generalization

Assumptions can mean trouble with family, friends, and most importantly, romantic partners. They are considered to be the termites of the relationship because they eat the foundation of it. Most of our assumptions are useless and only cause jealousy.

The society has basically generalized the standards of beauty, success, and achievement. It is so easy now more than ever to look at someone who "looks better than you" based on the society's standards and become envious. If such a person happens to be of the same gender as you and you spot them talking to your partner, then you become jealous. Your insecurity strikes. You forget that every person has their own tastes and preferences. Furthermore, you have set an idea of how relationships should be; hence, if your partner attempts to divert from the standards you feel they should maintain, you tend to become jealous.

We tend to possess assumptions about the behaviors of our partners and the intentions behind these behaviors, and we also assume that we behave in a certain way because that is how it should be. This is especially evident in the generalizations that "men should do this" or "women in the relationship should do this."

For instance, if you believe that your partner (man) should help out in the kitchen to show that they are really into you while, on the other hand, your partner does not believe that a man should be helping in the kitchen, you may develop a feeling of insecurity. Another example is a case where your partner tries to contact you to know what you would like to eat so that they could get it from the store on their way home but with no avail. In this case, they end up getting something for themselves and none for you. When they get to where you are, you might get furious and assume that they do not care about your own needs and that they selfishly think about themselves when in reality your partner may not have wanted to bring something that would not make you happy. Your partner may also assume that you are unreasonable and overly emotional.

When led by assumptions and generalizations, you tend to judge why they are behaving the way they are behaving. You fill your mind with negative thoughts, and you think that a perceived rival (third party) is keeping your partner engaged. You will become jealous over insignificant things just because you believe that according to society, your partner should behave in a certain manner. Our assumptions basically project on how we relate with our partners.

**Expectations**

People get into relationships and expect their partner to behave in a certain way. The truth is that jealousy is most often caused by unrealistic and insatiable expectations about a relationship. People tend to assume that feelings are true facts; hence, they equate their expectations to what should actually be the real case.

We all have our own ideas of romance, connections, passion, destiny, and intimacy. We have expectations on how our relationships should be. Some of our ideas have formed since childhood. Others are formed by listening to our peers and the media on what they expect from a relationship. As different as we all are, people's expectations vary. Some people think that, in a healthy relationship, people should fall in love quickly while others think that it should take time. Also, some people think that the relationship they are in is predestined to lead to marriage and eternity, while others do not think about marriage when they enter a relationship. To them, a relationship that leads to marriage and a bond that lasts forever requires hard work, and this is determined as time goes by.

Usually, people's expectations are reflected in how they attach to their partners. They are reflected in how they view themselves and view their partners.

Some people enter a relationship with a high level of independence while others expect to spend every time with their partner. Some people expect too much, and they assume that their expectations will be met in the relationship. In fact, some people expect that a relationship will cure their childhood scars or that it is a path to self-actualization and enlightenment.

While no one should settle for being treated poorly in a relationship, the main problem with expectations is that you are always going to be watching what your partner is doing to meet your wild expectations and not your contribution to the relationship. You assume that your partner should do everything to please you; hence, you definitely get jealous when they do something that does not make you happy. You tend to criticize everything they do because they are not living up to your expectations, and you become frustrated eventually when everything they do does not match your expectations. Maybe you belong to the "falling in love quickly" group, and your partner belongs to the "true bond of love takes time" group. You will always be jealous and insecure, and this will cause you problems in your relationship.

## Investment in the Relationship

Now, every relationship requires an investment of time, sacrifices, efforts, and even money. You have to compromise part of your lifestyle to accommodate your partner and make the relationship work. However, most often, it turns out that some people become too invested in the relationship than their partner.

Many people invest in their relationship to make it work, and it often flows from the assumptions and expectations that they have about how an excellent relationship should be and how things should be done. Also, it is hard to find two people in a relationship who love each other equally, and that is perfectly fine. The problem comes when the imbalance of love makes one think that they are the only ones putting in effort or like they are taking the relationship seriously alone. Most of the people who tend to get overly jealous are because they invested too much and their investment was not replicated. However, it is entirely one thing to hope for a certain outcome, and the actual results that you get are another. Most often, you are likely to be overrun with negative thoughts of jealousy and insecurity. You feel like you are slowly losing your partner if your partner does not invest in the relationship with the same energy. For instance, a man who invests a lot of money taking care of the lady he is in a relationship with would feel jealous if the lady does not show 100 percent love for them. On the flip side, a lady who invests her time and effort to perform all house chores for the man would feel jealous if the man does not love her more.

**Aging**

Aging has become a common reason for jealousy in most people. The freshness in the younger skin can easily make someone to long for what they once were. It is easy to get sad over younger people who seem to be doing better than you or are more physically appealing than you are. This is worse when we begin to think about how we wasted our time back then, thinking we are not strong enough, attractive enough, or smart enough. Now we have grown older, and we have more serious challenges to handle. We attempt to look at our pictures, and we admire how we were when their age. We cannot help but feel bad about ourselves and feel jealous of such people. For instance, it is possible for one to feel jealous of a situation where their partner works with a younger person (perceived rival) who appears better than them. They would do anything to have their partner or the perceived rival transferred for them to not work together.

Aging also gets us worried and makes us think that everything should be aligned at a particular age. It makes us think that we should be settled with a lifetime partner. If our partner seems to be pleased by a younger person, we tend to become jealous. We develop insecurities that our partner might leave us for this younger person. We start viewing ourselves as failures because we feel like we are running out of time to enjoy dating. Most people have their friendships secured by thirty years. An above-thirty individual who finds their partner developing some likeness for a younger person may be tempted to feel rejection based on age.

## Chapter 4: How Jealousy Hurts You

Negative emotions are part of the human experience. Jealousy is in itself a negative emotion because you constantly desire to have something that you don't have, to own something that someone else owns, to change the state of affairs and make things match your pattern of thinking. Jealousy shows you that you do not have enough to offer, that you can't achieve something, and that you're probably not lovable. However, psychologists have consistently proven that negative thoughts harm us and can become detrimental to our ability to coexist peacefully with others (Batey, May, and Andrade, 2010). Negative emotions are the source of other negative things in our lives because they affect the mind-body connection. For instance, they lead us into anger, anxiety, sadness, stress, and even depression.

Emotional health is paramount for most of the things you do in your life. Your body responds to your overall attitude—how you feel, think, and act.

Whenever you're under stress or anxiety, for instance, you tend to misjudge things. You tend to make decisions that may have been made better had you relaxed. Most of these decisions end up as regrets in the future. The primary response to jealousy is the feeling of unworthiness and hopelessness, which results in physical manifestations such as shaking, increased heart rates, and crying. It is a natural reaction to the feeling of being threatened.

Further physical manifestations of the insecurity and pain because of jealousy include sleep deprivation and lack of proper feeding. The hurtfulness of a romantic relationship is a major cause for the misery that people go through, where the stress leads you to stay up long nights, crying and trying to find answers to most often "helpless" questions. Also, most people have shown the effects of being unable to eat when they are feeling hurt and stressed.

An intense feeling of jealousy exposes you to stress because you engage your mind into thinking about how best you can change how things are. You ask yourself why your partner does not seem to realize that you need attention. You wonder what will happen to you if you part with them, and you ask yourself why your partner "despises" you. Instead of focusing on the positive side of the relationship and what you bring to the table, you obsess over the things you might be lacking. You develop a feeling of sadness because you always imagine that your partner is deliberately hurting you. You even tend to question why the universe is so unfair to you.

Now, these feelings reflect in how you relate with your partner. It is almost impossible to conceal your negativity, especially when it has to do with the person that you adore the most. In effect, you behave in such a manner that shows that you are anxious about every move they make since you think that they are out here trying to hurt you. You tend to become possessive, and you want to monitor each of their moves. The more you try, the worse it becomes for you. The more you feel like a failure, the less happy you become.

Happiness is among the requirements for a good daily functioning of your brain. Once you are happy, you are able to embrace anything that comes your way from an objective point of view. Sadness, anxiety, and stress make you look at everything from a subjective point of view. When left unmanaged, these emotions are detrimental to your relationship.

Jealousy leads to ungratefulness since, instead of focusing on what we have, we focus on what we do not have. By envying the good things in other people's lives, you become hateful and wish for them to lose it all so that you can be at an advantage yourself. You hold grudges for the third parties (perceived rivals) while you should not. Instead of losing, such people even tend to gain more, which discourages you even more. This denies you peace of mind and lowers your esteem even more. At the social scene, you appear withdrawn, and you do not want to associate with others who may not seem to understand your situation. Withdrawing from the social setup only directs you into more misery because you lose the chance to indulge in activities that can keep you happy.

Most importantly, jealousy is directly connected to anger. Anger is one of the emotions that we learned early enough as children to be able to control the attention we get from people. Our parents and teachers would give us harsh words or punishments to get our attention and to control our behaviors. Typically, it caught our attention when someone was angry at us. As we grow up, we do not necessarily forget this tactic. However, this pattern does not work in relationships, not especially today.

A jealous person may assume that being angry toward their partner is paramount to grab their attention. While our intellectual nature makes us aware that we have to behave differently, we tend to follow our falsified belief that anger will push someone to behave differently. Most often, your partner will withdraw from you.

It is emotionally unpleasing to show irrational anger. Therefore, anger hurts you because you do not attain a positive result at the end of the day; instead, your anger pushes your partner away from you. It also hurts your partner to part with you, but they had to because they could not handle your anger issues.

Anger never solves a problem. In fact, it is the beginning of many problems. If left unmanaged, anger easily turns into criminality where you can harm yourself or your partner. For instance, you can steal cash as an effort of pleasing your partner, and you can even fight them if they seem not to be listening to your concerns. In fact, there are numerous cases of the crimes of passion where jealous partners become irrational and commit homicides. People have reacted to the cases they perceived as threats with fury, such as suspecting that their partners are unfaithful. It is only long after committing crimes of passion that they realize that they had misjudged the situation and that the partner had not been cheating. Suicide cases are also common as a result of jealousy when people fail to see their worth for not being loved "as they should" by their partner. Although the results of jealousy are not exactly murderous, such cases are evidence of how strong jealousy as an emotion can be.

# Chapter 5: Why Jealousy Drives Your Partner Away

Expecting your partner to conform to your values, wishes, and beliefs is one of the most detrimental results of jealousy. This never works. Instead, it drives your partner further and further away from you. Jealous people often come off as irrational, troubled, controlling, and dangerous people. Given the free will to choose, no one wants to associate with someone who has such traits, lest they spread the negativity to them. Jealousy, especially in a romantic relationship, brings suspicion and pain. Moreover, conflict is likely to arise. It is no surprise that jealousy has been largely linked by research to dissatisfaction in a romantic relationship. And truth be told, no one wants to be with a person who never appreciates whatever they try to bring to the table. Jealousy breeds an insecure style of attachment, and it shows your partner the negative side of you all the time. Instead of having friendly chats, for instance, you always question why they are doing what they are doing.

In its basic form, jealousy is an emotion that gives us a natural response of wanting to protect what we deem ours. Rather than being positively and reasonably protective, jealousy tends to balloon really quickly, and before you know it, you are acting in a controlling and selfish manner. You always assume things that are not even existent (such as a friendly chat) as a sign of an affair. You even think that when your partner is working up late, they are having an affair. Entertaining such thoughts even drives you to put your partner under tests to assess their faithfulness or how much they love you. If your partner realizes that you are testing them, even the most rational person will not take it lightly. They would not want to be followed and monitored like a child is monitored by their parents. No one wants to be in "prison" in a world where they have all the chances to be free.

Also, constantly looking for assurance may be annoying to your partner. The foundation of a healthy relationship, after all, is trust and mutual respect. If you cannot respect the privacy and confidentiality of your partner, then they may not want to associate with you. If you have to go behind their back, then they cannot trust you in other things. You do not expect someone to drop all their lifestyle, friends, or values at a go just like the way you don't expect someone to ask you to drop yours. Do not try to change entirely who a person is. Doing this will not make you succeed; instead, you only make them distance themselves from you.

Accusing your partner of cheating on unfounded evidence is among the ugly instances that they may not be able to tolerate. They may tolerate it in a short while, but in the long run, they will get tired and withdraw. One of the things you need to know in dating is that getting honest remarks and answers to your jealous questions are not always easy. Your partner may not tell you directly that you are jealous, but they may just step aside to let you realize your negative attitude and perhaps change it for the better. The way you behave when jealous shows that you have already jumped into conclusions and are now putting a stamp on your predetermined answer.

If your bulk thoughts are your jealousy feelings, this sends them the message that it is not really safe being so close to you. This affects your ability to get intimate because you can't let them free and enjoy any moment. The intimacy that lacks passion and always appears like one person does not concentrate does not last for long. One of the core factors that make partners look forward to getting intimate with each other is the passion that each of them displays toward each other. Unfortunately, a jealous person cannot display this passion.

Also, if your way of thinking revolves around jealousy, you cannot hold a meaningful conversation with your partner. Talking only about your feelings is boring. Your partner cannot look forward to telling you something that happened in their day because of your absurd reactions and mostly because you are not a good listener.

However, one of the key things that keep a relationship going is having a meaningful conversation. This does not have to revolve around any of your feelings; it could be about an investment or a project or even about the current news. If your partner cannot have a friend in you to discuss with any matter, they will be forced to pull away and maybe look for someone else whom they can hold conversations with.

One of the key ingredients of a meaningful conversation is listening skills, whereby you get to hear from the other person's point of view. Also, your partner may keep secrets from you because they are afraid of the reaction they will get from disclosing some information since you seem to be spinning every bit of information and use it against them. Your reactions in the past teach them that they can hardly tell you stuff even if they did nothing wrong. It becomes hard for them to know what makes you happy and what makes you sad or insecure. Once secrets start piling, the relationship begins to assume a downward trend, which is nearly impossible to recover from. Secrets do not last long before they are discovered, and once again, you learn that your partner had not been honest with you. This creates a painful cycle that never ends and eventually drives away your partner.

If you realize that your partner is walking away because they are getting tired of your behavior, the first thing to do is to admit that you are jealous. You have to admit that you have a serious problem, then adapt mechanisms that will amend and not break the relationship further. You can rest guaranteed that most of the problems that occur in relationships today are based on jealousy. You do not expect someone to stay even when you are treating them like a suspect and an enemy every time when, in reality, they are supposed to be your best friends. People who dare to admit this and take corrective measures always experience more happiness in their relationships.

# Chapter 6: How to Track and Control Your Emotions

As mentioned in the previous chapter, jealousy is an involuntary feeling that occurs to us when we feel insecure or basically concerned about something with our partner. We mainly feel jealous when we see someone else with something that we don't have. This is especially worse when that thing is a natural endowment, such as the physical appearance of another person.

In human nature, no one has it all. We all lack something that other people have. At times, you will have money and no time to spend it. Other times, you will be broke but have all the time. In another case, however, you will have a lot of possessions but lack peace of mind. When we lack what someone else has at a certain moment, that is the point we begin to become envious, and if we have no control over this feeling, it becomes jealousy. This is not exceptional in relationships. You will be envious of a third party (a perceived rival) for something they have and that you lack in. You might also be jealous about your partner because you think that they are better than you and more privileged because it seems like they have no remorse when they hurt you and like they intentionally do things to hurt you.

While it is normal to feel envious, preventing the feeling of envy from turning you into a jealous animal determines the success of your relationship. It determines how you process and handle information about your partner, how well you hold a conversation, and how well the two of you relate. Therefore, it is paramount to track and control your emotions at all times to avoid coming off as an unfriendly and irrational partner.

The first thing you should know is that feelings are not facts. What may be true for you may not be true for another person. It is all about the perspective from which you look at things. Sometimes, we tend to forget to separate our feelings from facts. We fail to ascertain that whatever we are feeling is true, and we base our decisions and actions on the flawed feelings and assumptions.

For instance, just because you feel like you are not attractive enough does not mean you are not. Just because you feel like someone is deliberately ignoring you does not mean that it's true. Also, if someone ever humiliated you by calling you a loser, that doesn't mean that you are a loser. Therefore, it is possible that your jealousy results from the thoughts that are filtered through your feelings and personal understanding of what may not be true.

Being able to separate feelings from facts is entirely useful in managing jealousy. There is a fine line between acknowledging the truth of our feelings and not projecting them onto our surroundings. Being entitled about your feelings is the same as being self-righteous, and it is entirely destructive to a relationship.

Yes, it is your world, and it matters how you feel, but the universe does not care. With or without your feelings, life goes on. The moment you realize that your feelings of jealousy and insecurity may not always be facts and that projecting them onto your partner is detrimental to your relationship, you will want to find out if there is a way to manage your emotions. The truth is, you can manage your emotions and solve issues peacefully with your partner.

Moreover, realizing that the greatest enemy of every person is themselves can help you. One of the most valuable pieces of advice you will come across is that "your greatest enemy is your inner self." This does not have to be the case. Your inner self can be your best friend or your worst enemy. Every thought, action, and behavior is dictated by your inner person. For instance, you know the right things to eat, but you choose to either ignore or follow. Either of these decisions has implications for your health.

We are all bound to face moments of frustration and desperation in life, but giving in to these feelings is the worst thing we can do. Fortunately, there is a way in which we can be aware of this monster within us and overpower its demoralizing power. You can learn to silence your worst fear and appear as the most courageous and confident person. You can always calm your insecurities and negative feelings toward your partner.

The following is a guide on how you can do this:

**Stop Being a Perfectionist**

The truth is that perfectionists tend to get jealous. It may sound good to say that you are a perfectionist in a job interview, but this is detrimental to the greater part of your life, especially in managing relationships and failure. If you are a perfectionist, you do not expect your romantic partner to make mistakes. You are easily offended by mistakes, and you have fed your mind with all the attributes of perfectionism that you think is appropriate. You have extremely high standards and overly evaluate and criticize yourself.

As a perfectionist, you will always expect that your partner judges you harshly and that you have to display perfection to secure ultimate approval. Some of the mental problems associated with perfectionism are stress, anxiety, and depression. Perfectionism has been largely linked to young people. We are overly fed by social networking sites with things that are perfect. They always show us how an ideal life should be. However, we do not get to see the real side of the people we interact with online. Do not expect your partner to be perfect, and do not think that your partner will love you only if you are perfect.

Learn to understand that nothing is perfect. No one is perfect, and neither can anyone be perfect. Embrace your flaws and understand that your partner has their own flaws as well. Then learn how to utilize your strengths to address these weaknesses. In this way, you can always avoid being jealous over things you probably cannot change.

## Perform a Personality Test to Understand Yourself Better

It is natural for humans to want to know who they really are. Try to take a personality test. The results will uncover your real traits, and you will likely find out what aspect in your life and relationship you need to work on. Personality tests help you connect with others cordially by making you more aware of yourself. You might discover things about yourself that you might otherwise be unaware of. You will realize what drains your energy and what fills up your spirit, and this can be used to understand why you react the way you do to envious triggers. You can learn to cope with these emotions and control them and not the other way around, and you can create happiness for yourself.

Personality quizzes are all over the internet today. It is almost impossible to check social media sites or go through websites without being prompted to take one. You should leverage this availability to perform one. In fact, most people perform them for fun, and they end up revealing nuggets of wisdom that help shed light on various aspects of their lives.

It might seem trivial, but the results of a personality test can go a long way in making your dating and relationship phase successful. It can help you determine who you can best be compatible with. You may be feeling jealous, insecure, and all other negativities toward your partner because you are not compatible with each other.

Results of a personality test help you understand other people better, and you will know how to handle their reactions. You can understand their perception of the various aspects of life. The most common mistake people commit in relationships is assuming that other people have the same views and opinions as them.

Essentially, a personality test is among the major ways through which you can understand how best you function. It is a major step into making your life and your relationship better.

## Keep a Journal to Track Your Emotions

Most successful people in history have kept journals that detail most aspects of their lives. Even though you do not see the need for one, a journal is among the most powerful tools through which you can succeed in any journey of life. While you may think that journals are best for investments, studies, and other major projects, journals are crucial for tracking your moods and emotions on a day-to-day basis. Keeping a mood-tracking journal has great benefits that you can begin to enjoy instantly.

Assuming that you have already made a decision to stop treating your feelings as facts and that you are willing to work on yourself, a journal should become your best friend. First, writing releases your daily stresses because it helps you relive the moments you experienced in an environment. It can also boost your esteem and make you feel happier.

Overall, journaling helps to calm your fears and prioritize problems in daily life. Through the journal, you can easily track down your triggers of jealousy and establish proper ways of handling them. It gives you a window into identifying when negative thoughts seem to cross your mind and have positive self-talk. When you feel too much of the negative feelings caused by jealousy, including insecurity, stress, and fear of loss, you can easily turn to your journal to try identifying what is causing these feelings.

However, it is not just the writing but also the thinking and feeling what you are writing about that matter in journaling. You do not just state your feelings plainly, but you tell your personal story of what you were thinking at the moment you had a certain mood.

The journal serves as a good reminder of the mistakes you have done in the past, and it also helps you to decipher the most probable reason you did so. This helps you in your retrospection to guide you on the best behavior to assume going forward. Furthermore, there are various ways to journal your moods, including keeping a notebook or using one of the various journal apps.

The best tip for maintaining a helpful journal is to keep it easy. Do not write fiction stories. Write every day if you can and let the words you use to flow freely. You can be assured that it will help bring order to your life and your relationship even when it feels like it is full of chaos. Most importantly, find some moments to revisit the journal, especially whenever something makes you uncomfortable.

**Improve Your Emotional Intelligence**

We cannot deny that emotions are powerful. Whenever you are happy, for instance, you have the confidence to take on the world without anything stopping you. On the flip side, when you are sad or anxious, you experience the opposite attitude. Every emotion influences us in different ways. The problem comes when we allow emotions to get a hold of us in a bad way because the excess of any emotion leads to disastrous decisions and actions if not controlled.

Also referred to as EQ, the concept of emotional intelligence has become increasingly relevant as the demands from people's lives exert so much pressure to them and reduce their ability to form meaningful relationships with others. Understanding this concept helps you to recognize emotions, understand the powerful effect these emotions can have, and be able to apply this knowledge in your behavior and thinking. Learning how you react to various situations can help you to improve your relations with other people. This comes in handy in your relationship as well since you can identify when you feel jealous and how to address this feeling.

Eve after performing personality tests and adapting a journal as your tool to track your emotions, it all boils down to how good you are at recognizing and dissecting these emotions to know what they mean for your relationship. People with low EQ tend to hold grudges. They get stressed easily, thus making assumptions and defending them vehemently. They often feel misunderstood. These are the major ways in which you react to your partner whenever jealousy strikes you.

To improve your EQ, try to be aware of your emotions and understand how they affect your functioning. Do you wish they could change or improve? Pause whenever you are experiencing the strong emotions to avoid saying or doing something that you might regret later.

Over time, identifying a feeling and pausing becomes your norm and builds your EQ. Also, remember to empathize with your partner by trying to think why they said what they said or did what they did. Considering their actions might make you realize that they may not have been deliberately hurting you. Finally, take every opportunity you have to learn. Whenever your partner criticizes you and points out some irrational jealousy-based things that you said or did, consider whatever there is to learn. Rather than taking feedback personally, consider negative feedback as what you might need to go over the hurdle that looks like a mountain of jealousy.

## Concentrate on the Things That Matter

The brain is one of the most powerful body organs. It is capable of processing tons of information based on what it is fed with. Then the brain controls your behavior, thinking, and attitude based on this information. Also, the brain has the capability to diminish poor behaviors and awaken strong behaviors. The brain is sensitive to being distracted, and this can drastically affect your productivity and performance. Interferences are either externally or internally induced.

The internal factors that may induce your brain are the thoughts that you store within your heart. The external factors are the triggers that you see in the external environment of your body. If you do not concentrate on the things that matter, you can easily lose your focus and give in to whatever is inducing your mind. This is what happens with jealousy. Whenever you lose your concentration on the positive bits of the relationship, any jealousy trigger carries away your emotions and leads you into poor decision-making. Most of the time, these triggers will win against you if you are not careful. The brain does not favor the conditions where you have mixed emotions, and most of the time, it is inclined toward the negative.

Rather than focusing on what you don't have or what your partner lacks, concentrate on the relationship itself and how the two of you handle conflicts. What are the common values between both of you? Focus on your sense of humor. Focus on how to be respectful, kind, and open, and even how to improve your deep friendship.

Do not look at the things that fade away, such as money and beauty. Instead, focus your mind on what you two are looking up to achieve in the near future. This will train your brain to focus on the positive aspects and use these to override the negative triggers that may be trying to distract you from the things that matter.

## Overcome Jealousy after Betrayal

One thing that you should know is that constantly nagging a spouse who once cheated but whom you forgave can lead them into cheating again or distancing themselves from you. While it is normal to feel jealous under a situation wherein your husband cheated and a child was born out of that event (which means your spouse keeps constant communication with the baby's mother), it is important to work on yourself and overcome the feeling of jealousy whenever it strikes.

Work on your feelings, no matter how hard this may be. As mentioned earlier, you should focus on the things that matter and learn to value the person that you are. As long as you are willing to continue with the relationship, you should ensure that you are at peace and the negative feelings are over. Failure to calm the fears and insecurities in you will lead you to follow your partner to ensure they do not hook up with the person they cheated with again. Do not invade their privacy because this only shows them that you do not trust them, and it might drive them away from you.

Try talking to your partner to share your feelings and fears. Provided they are willing to continue with the relationship and have expressed their remorse after cheating on you, you should continue trusting and working on your relationship through open communication.

This does not only apply to the betrayal of a current partner. If you were betrayed in your previous relationship or if you faced a rough time in your childhood because of betrayal, you should not take your fears and insecurities into your current relationship, hoping to make it a long-lasting bond. The best thing you can do is to take time to heal and take the courage to try again.

Not everyone is the same. Also, a person who once broke your trust can change and become a good person if you decide to start again and work on your bond. Essentially, you must be willing to shed away your baggage to be able to continue with a healthy relationship. You cannot be jealous over every little thing just because you have been betrayed in the past. One of the common misconceptions around is that you should not trust fully or that you should not give someone your whole heart and efforts. Carrying this attitude with you will only cause more pressure and expose the jealousy in you through your actions, thoughts, and behaviors.

You have to realize that building trust takes a lot of work, and couples who excel together have mastered the art of building trust and always working toward bettering their bond. You have to be each other's best friends for you to build the foundation of trust. Remember that you always get what you give. If you cultivate an attitude of not trusting, the ultimate result for this is heartbreak, adding onto the betrayal scar that you have never healed. You don't want to live a miserable life where you cannot last in a relationship.

## Overcome Your Inferiority Complex

The effort to overpower your inferiority complex, fears, and insecurities must come from the heart, lest it won't be successful. You must cultivate the willpower and determination for your efforts to continue in a positive direction. It takes a lot of discipline to control the emotion that shows you that you are not enough, not attractive enough, not successful enough, or not lovable enough.

Identify whether what you have always been ridiculed upon is rectifiable. Identify whether it does not make you stop from being yourself by adopting a covering image in order to please someone. Remember that you cannot do this for long, and you cannot live happily and peacefully if you keep pretending to be someone you are not. If it can't be changed, then take the first step of accepting that the situation is there.

For instance, if you always feel insecure because of physical shortcomings, you don't have to perform plastic surgery to be attractive to your partner. If you are comfortable with doing this without struggling financially and mentally, then you can go ahead and perform it to enhance your beauty. However, you don't have to "break the bank" to please someone.

In fact, most of the insecurities that we feel are not really noticeable to our partners. Understand that for the person to have gotten intimate with you and expressed their interest in being with you, you must have attracted them first. When beauty meets the eye, you want to know the person better, and it is usually what is in their heart that matters. Therefore, work on keeping your heart and mind at peace so that you can radiate beauty and intelligence all the time.

Of course, positive thinking is the best strategy to overcome your inferiority complex, but it is often hard to regard yourself highly when you have faced disappointments in every area for most of your life. It becomes really hard to employ positive thinking to cross to the other side. However, you have to make yourself understand that no one is superior to others.

It is only your environment surrounding you that makes you feel like you are really inferior. We are all gifted differently, and once you realize this, you do not allow anyone to turn you down based on what you are not good at. Also, you do not get jealous because someone else has something that you do not have. Appreciate that one strength that you possess and focus on it whenever envious feelings strike.

**Do Not Jump to Conclusions**

Abbreviated as JTC, jumping to conclusions is a representation of a bias in interpretation that leads us to assume that a situation bears harm for us. We face every emotionally difficult condition from a negative point, and we often conclude that it will have negative results for you. This is driven by the basic thought that other people are out there to hurt you. In the case of a relationship, you always assume that your partner is out there trying to hurt you.

Lack of trust makes you suspicious of everything that your partner does, and you hardly see the good in anything. There are numerous times when we are prompted to jump into conclusions, but this is one of the most detrimental aspects of a relationship. Whenever we see something odd, we are quick to assume that the person behind it is deliberately hurting us. It harms not only your relationship but also your mental wellness. Anxiety and threat anticipation are what cause someone to jump into conclusion. While your cognitive reaction is concluding something, it is paramount that you control whatever this conclusion directs you into saying or doing. It is always good to give your partner the benefit of the doubt rather than thinking the worst.

Therefore, cultivate in you an attitude that your partner wants the best for you. Unless you are really sure that you are dating a psycho, the first thought that comes to your mind when you notice something off with your partner should be to get to talk to them and hear from their side. Always strive to see the whole picture of a situation rather than relying on your one-sided view. Understand that your own illusions can lure you into concluding that something is true or that it exists while it doesn't. Realize that for a relationship to remain solid, every argument or conclusion reached should be based on solid evidence.

Jumping into conclusions will make you a loser from many ends. At the end of the day, you will drive your partner away by constantly accusing them based on your conclusions, and you will never learn how to deal with issues correctly. Even though you might eventually part with your partner because of your differences, your jumping into conclusions should not be a reason. You should focus on learning from every relationship experience that you encounter for you to become a better person. In fact, you should focus on being a better person for your partner's peace, happiness, and prosperity as well as your own.

## Understanding That No One Is Perfect

One of the common mistakes people make in life pertaining to social relationships is assuming that other people are perfect. One of the most thought-provoking questions you should ask yourself when you have such a tendency is "If I'm not perfect, how do I expect others to be perfect?" Do you make mistakes? Does this make you a bad person? Yes, you do make mistakes. And no, this does not make you a bad person.

Everyone makes mistakes. It all depends on how you handle their mistakes. The best approach to handling the mistakes of a partner is with gentleness and compassion. If you come out attacking them, they will try to counterattack. In fact, it is found in the Christian scriptures that harsh words stir up anger, but a gentle response turns away wrath. Even if your partner appears withdrawn, you should approach them calmly and learn whatever their problem is. Learn when the moment to best process information is. For instance, you may find that asking a personal question to your partner in the morning before starting their day will mess up their whole mood and the day.

You should not amplify your partner's mistakes to the point of harboring insecurities, jealousy, and fears that you shouldn't have and that will only hurt you and your relationship. When you accept that the human in them is bound to make mistakes and that not everything they do will make you happy, you can control your emotions whenever they seem to attack you.

# Chapter 7: Custom-Fit Approach to Jealousy for Different Couples

As mentioned in chapter 2, the major reason why people tend to be jealous is generalizing. People tend to make assumptions that couples should behave in a certain manner. And when a partner fails to live up to these generalized standards, jealousy strikes right in.

Also, some people think that everything their partners do should be to make them happy. However, why allow such an outrageous attitude to stay in your mind? It will only keep you unhappy and jealous at all times. Why not understand that everyone has different interests and that this does not exclude you and your partner?

For instance, people tend to think that just because they do not like loud music, their partner will have to keep the volume low at all times. This is one of the most destructive perspectives in relationships. It takes two people willing to work together to find common ground. It is all about compromise, learning to accept each other, and trying to change to accommodate your partner. However, these things do not happen overnight. Also, you have to understand that your partner cannot possibly change all their behaviors and points of view just because you "like" or "dislike" something.

As we have already established, jealousy is not entirely bad. In fact, it is important because it signals that some of your emotional needs are unmet. However, whether you are seeking security from your partner or assurance that you are the top priority, you should not let jealousy take over you and control your attitude toward your partner. You should endeavor to establish a technique that suits you and your partner in handling envious feelings before they turn into destructive jealousy.

All relationships are different. Whatever works for one couple that seems successful in taming jealousy may not work for you and your partner. After all, you are jealous for different reasons, and there are different levels to which such jealousy triggers can be eliminated to bring the relationship back on track.

**Understand Your Partner's Love Language**

Understanding your partner's love language is one of the most ignored yet valuable ingredients in a relationship. As proposed by Dr. Gary Chapman around two decades ago, the love languages mostly appear in five different forms. These are the words of affirmation, quality time, receiving gifts, physical touch, and acts of service. These languages differ from person to person, and understanding the different meanings these languages have for your partner is core to building a healthy relationship. They describe how someone feels appreciated and loved or how they would rather have it. Our individual personalities make us feel loved differently. We tend to display all these languages but on different levels. There are people to whom gifts come first while words of affirmation are last on the list. To others, acts of service top the list while physical touch is the last.

Gaining insight into what means the most to you and your partner is important in handling jealousy. For instance, for a person who values quality time, giving them their undivided attention and engaging in various activities together with them will make them feel loved. If you realize that your partner values quality time, you would know that distractions (such as phone calls when you are together or failure to listen whenever they are talking) will hurt them the most and trigger jealousy. Even though this may not be your top priority, you may want to sacrifice for your partner and give them what they love. It shows that you are dearly expressing heartfelt love and commitment to them.

Furthermore, if your partner's love language is "acts of service," they would feel loved if you contemplate on helping out with the things that are weighing down on them. Things such as showing laziness with carrying out your share of chores are devastating to them, and they become irritable. Furthermore, if your partner loves words of affirmation, they enjoy hearing from you and being assured regularly how you love them. This is what makes them feel loved and secure in the relationship. It is not like they are too needy, but if they do not regularly get these words from you, they feel unloved and insecure.

This also applies to gifts and physical touch. If you do not display affection through touching your partner who considers this their top priority, they begin developing insecurities and feeling unloved. If you go for long without gifting your partner who values gifts, they begin to feel unloved. Take note that gifts do not have to be so huge or so expensive for an understanding person to appreciate. Gifting entails even small items but which makes someone feel loved.

Maybe knowing your partner's love language is what you need to really save the relationship. In fact, it is an interesting practice to take together as you realize the different things that make both of you happy. Learning each other's language will allow you to communicate your needs more even if it means to be complimented when you're well-dressed without having to ask them. It will also show them what they can do to keep you from being jealous or insecure in the relationship. It will enhance your thoughtfulness and their thoughtfulness too.

Therefore, learning these languages will have overall positive implications for your relationship. Not only will you be able to know how to show and receive love better, but you will also know when your partner is being overwhelmed by the feeling of being unloved and when they are giving up even when it doesn't feel fair for you.

## Communicative Responses

Since romantic jealousy comprises of complex feelings, thoughts, and actions, communicative responses are important to reduce doubtfulness, repair the relationship, and make it sustainable. There are general behaviors and interactive responses that you can use as a couple to boost each other's confidence in the relationship. What matters in the kind of response you use is the emotion displayed by your partner.

Often, jealousy is associated with anger. Hence, using an aggressive communicative response may stir an already angry person up, and this will not be good for either of you. To determine the best communicative response to use, you should seek to understand critical things about the relationship and your partner. These include the commitment level of both of you and how your partner's emotional state is like.

Falling in love feels all fun, and in the early phase of the relationship, both of you are unstoppable in everything concerning each other. However, reality begins to settle in, and you start realizing things about your partner that you were "blind" about. I emphasize that it is good to ensure that you are on the same page with your partner from the beginning. You do not have to "follow the flow" and realize six months into it that they value being sexually exclusive with you while you are into long-term relationships all along.

If this happens, you are always going to appear more jealous than they are, and no amount of communication will bring you on the same level. It is important to know their perception of dating and relationships, expectation about the relationship, and their view about the future. Also, you should check from time to time to be certain about the desires and dreams about your relationship. You should strive to ensure that you are on the same commitment level to avoid being carried away by comparisons between couples and what you think they do better than your partner and you.

For instance, you might be thinking that your partner is not supposed to really entertain other people into their space because you are with them, while they are only with you for having fun and nothing serious. In such a case, you will know how to treat your partner and stop being jealous over things they do not deem wrong. Also, you will be able to talk to them and agree on what can be tolerated and what cannot be tolerated of each other. Most importantly, you should aim at being at peace and not having to feel insecure or unloved by someone whom you are not on the same level of commitment.

Also, your partner may be going through an emotional state. You know that do when they distance themselves, when they are not talking too much, when they are working harder than they normally are, or even when they appear lazy. They may not have to tell you that they are in an emotional state. It is upon you to realize when they are in this emotional state based on your deep understanding of them as a person.

Just as you realize the simplest of emotions, such as happiness or sorrow, you should be able to detect when your partner is jealous. This does not equal to another person; hence, a partner should be studied differently. Understand that the purpose of communication is to bring some mutual understanding of an issue that was indifferent between partners. However, communication cannot be effective if one of you cannot comprehend and use this information for the benefit of the relationship. It would be meaningless to keep communicating with a person whose behavior you do not understand. This is discussed in details later.

## Understanding Each Other's Philosophy of Love and a Healthy Relationship

It hurts to imagine that the person you love the most is causing you more pain than joy. However, this can happen all because people have a different perspective on love, and your partner may have different views on what makes a relationship work. They may be trying to make you happy, but you do not think that a relationship is supposed to be this way.

It is important to understand each other's idea of a healthy relationship and to respect each other's background, including how one was brought up and the previous dating experiences they have had. These experiences will shape up their perspective on dating. Constantly talk to each other to see what both of you feel makes a relationship work. This can help you set boundaries and limits and eliminate the chances of being made jealous. Most of the jealousy cases couples fight about are preventable if you know each other's philosophy on love. You might be surprised to find that the reason your partner parted with the previous person or maybe parted ways with a certain friend is that of jealousy on either party.

It is not good to assume that the way that you view the world is the same way that your partner does. Understanding each other's perspective helps you to accept, love, and date a person for who they really are. Be a listening partner, and do not be afraid to ask questions to which you feel like you need answers.

Rather than showing your partner that you can only accept a part of their feelings and beliefs, consider their points of view (POV) as opportunities to learn more. Rather than seeing these differences as potential conflict grounds, focus on helping your partner see things from another perspective, and encourage them to learn as well.

One of the greatest pieces of advice in a relationship is that you are constantly trying to make each other become better people. Your partner will feel more safe and secure when you do not have to challenge their points of view. As such, they will open up to you more and let you access the deeper parts of their hearts. They will be willing to share information because they know they can trust you with the information. They know that you will not use it to justify your actions, hold it against them, or become jealous because they seem to know and do better than you. If both of you understand each other on a mature level, you will no longer need to amplify your feelings in order to be heard. You will be calm when expressing something that bothers you, and you can be assured of getting an honest answer.

**Overcoming Assumptions**

First, you have to realize that you are making assumptions in a relationship once you think that you know how they are feeling and thinking. This never works because you are now judging them from your own perspective and unique value system. Your partner's true thoughts and feelings can only be known to you if they tell you, which will happen if you engage in a meaningful conversation. To ensure that you are not making an assumption, you always have to ensure that you have facts. Be keen on statements that are thrown at you such as "Why are you putting words in my mouth?" or "Why are you trying to tell me what I think?" because they show that you are always making assumptions.

We already know that assumptions escalate the negative impact of envious feelings. They create a constant sense of tension, and they lead a person to shut down because the assuming partner does not try to connect with their partner or be receptive of their side of the story. It is important to challenge your assumptions to avoid driving your partner away.

To do this, make sure to ask your partner anything that doesn't seem to add up from your perspective. Check in with them to understand their feelings and thoughts. Clarify whatever they said to get what they meant. Ensure that you understand each other fully whenever making plans or decisions. Be sure to establish the right time and the right way to talk to them, lest it appears rude or inappropriate. Also, be accountable for any of the things that your partner points out. If they felt you were disrespectful or hurtful, be sure to claim responsibility. When both partners do their part of claiming responsibility, they are able to establish a common ground.

You have to respond to the feeling of jealousy in a way that is adaptive rather than harmful. Although we cannot prevent bad things from happening to us, there are always two ways in which you can respond to these when they happen. You can choose to sit down and pity your life, or you can alternatively accept that it happened and look for the best way to avoid it.

The most successful people in history did not live a journey without any problem. Even the people whose marriages have lasted for a long time were not perfect partners who did not make mistakes. Neither did they live in an idealized world where no problems occurred. In any journey that you take in life, there are bound to be mistakes, challenges, and problems. What matters is how you approach such, and that is what differentiates between a winner and a loser. Successful people always choose the right approach to handling problems. They possess the right attitude. A great philosopher once argued that "a bad attitude is like a flat tire." What this means is that with a bad attitude, you cannot go anywhere. You cannot move past your current position. Instead, you become a retrogressive person whose main focus is on the negative and unhelpful side.

Obviously, you are not going to be gaga over each other with your partner every day. However, who says that there won't be lows and downs? In fact, partners who ever agree in everything live a "boring" life. There need to be times that stir you up and push you out of the comfort zone. What matters is how such situations are handled.

It is good to understand that we can always plan for the good times and be ready to handle the bad times.

## Escaping the Threat of Communication Technologies and Social Media

In the modern world, the internet and the mobile phone have become among the greatest enemies to partners in a relationship. Whether you like to admit it or not, these technologies play a crucial role in relationships today. It is easy to become jealous over something as simple as a compliment on a picture posted on Instagram. Also, you become jealous when your partner indulges too much in social media whenever you are together such that their attention for you is divided. It might make you a little envious to imagine that your partner is getting the attention of other people in the social scene and is spending most of the time on social media. One thing that couples should realize is that it is okay if one partner attracts social media attention. It only shows that their partner is attractive or is making an impact in the lives of other people through the content they share. Instead of getting jealous, one should understand this and be supportive.

However, there are certain things that partners should do to ensure that social media does not cause jealousy, which can ruin their relationship. Openness is core to this. Partners should be able to share and let their significant others know about aspects such as admirers instead of hiding every direct message (DM) to avoid your partner finding. What matters is not what other people say to you but how you respond to them. Also, do not over-engage with other people on social media, especially if the content is not friendly for a relationship. You should be able to draw the lines on the comments you make on social media to avoid displaying your life, your love life, or your partner on a negative light. Most importantly, both of you should not over-indulge on social media to the point that even when you are at dinner, in bed, out on a date, or any other time you are together, you are busy with your phone, responding to social media messages and comments. Unless it is on work terms, social media should be spared for when the two of you are not together.

## Working as a Team

Generally, teamwork promotes a winning spirit. This does not only happen in the workplace or learning institutions, where people are placed together to work on a project. It also applies to relationships. In fact, a relationship should be considered as a lifetime project, and teamwork is the core requisite.

Relationships can be compared to a three-legged race. If you try pushing ahead without the collaboration of the two of you, both of you are bound to fail miserably. However, when you push together, you are stronger, and you do well. Working as a team eliminates the chances of jealousy because you do not think that the other person is out there hurting you. Furthermore, you have more security because you are sure that if any of you tries to mess up, then they hurt a project that you are running together, and both of you will feel the implications.

In a relationship, sometimes people tend to forget to apply teamwork; instead, they start considering their partners as their enemy or their competitor. This attitude is what paves the way for jealousy and insecurity because you think that your partner just wants to do better than you and do not care to hurt you.

You will be amazed how emotionally transparent you can become if you work as a team. The results you can gain from this are great. When you realize a weakness in your partner, you are quick to find a good way to help them improve because you are looking out for each other and you do not want either of you to mess your teamwork.

This makes communications seamless, and every challenge is handled easily. Understand that maybe a mean comment that your partner made did not mean to hurt you. Take all challenges positively and utilize the chance for growth. Most importantly, remember that although these are the fundamental guidelines of teamwork, each team has a different goal and different elements that work for them. Therefore, be sure to create your own long-term goal and build a team that is suited to achieve this goal. Communicate and clarify everything you feel and think. Coordinate your efforts of making each other better people.

However, there are other things that you need to add to your relationship to make sure that the above approaches work:

1. **Be together for the right reasons:** You cannot expect to be together with your partner if you are not together for the right reasons. It will be so hard for you to try building a custom-fit approach to jealousy for you and your partner if the two of you cannot collaborate.

2. **Have realistic expectations about romance and relationships:** If you cannot lower your high expectations and keep them at a reasonable level, then you cannot succeed in trying to tailor your thoughts together to establish what works for you.

3. **Respect for each other:** It might look weird, but respect is way much better than love or communication. While communication appears to be the cure for all disagreements in a relationship, it is hard to communicate effectively if you have no mutual respect for each other.

4. **Openness about the things that hurt:** If you feel the need to bottle up your feelings for the sake of not being judged or appearing as weak, know that you are setting yourself up to living a miserable life in that relationship.

5. **Establish that both of you are healthy:** If you are to build a healthy relationship, then it has got to be with a healthy person, and you have got to be healthy yourself. Focus on being healthy to absorb all the things that come with a relationship before you identify if your partner is ready for this.

6. **Embrace the growth and change that both of you experience along the way:** You are not going to remain the same way as when you began dating with your partner. You two will change physically, mentally, and spiritually. You may have more wealth and riches. You may increase weight. You may become more learned. You are going to deal with deeper issues, such as marriage, having children, or investing together. You are going to learn more about your partner from time to time. These changes count as part of the journey, and they are necessary at different ages. You have to be flexible and understand your partner through all these changes. Also, you have to be aware of the changes occurring inside of you so that you can learn how to bring the changes to the table. The change should not take the better part of you or your partner. It should be for the good of both of you.

7. **Conflict resolution:** For every couple to be successful, both parties must adopt the best techniques to present their points during an argument. Most of the partners that tend to break up are those that do things such as criticizing a partner. Do not criticize them through statements such as "What you just did was so stupid." Also, do not be defensive and always shift blames through arguments such as "Were it not for your lateness, I wouldn't have done this." Also, avoid stonewalling by withdrawing from an argument and ignoring what your partner has to say. Most importantly, avoid holding your partner into contempt by making them feel inferior during an argument.

8. **Forgive, forgive, and forgive!** Weird as it may seem, even the most successful people are not able to resolve all their issues. You have to accept that you cannot change your partner and that there are going to be times when they bore you to the core. You have to be ready to forgive

and let it go away. Most importantly, you should try to identify what bothers either of you the most and how you can find a solution to it.

Essentially, these are quick tips that have worked for all couples, and they must be observed for you to effectively deal with jealousy or any other mishap in the relationship.

# Chapter 8: How to Identify Triggers of Jealousy

To this point, we have identified that jealous has to do with the mind of a person, especially how you interpret something or a situation that happens. Take, for instance, you are sitting with him in a park, and all is going fine, both of you enjoying your time. Then out of nowhere, a certain girl appears. She is smartly dressed than you, and she looks more beautiful than you. Then she starts talking to him. You are fully and consciously focused at them—how she looks at him and how he smiles at her. You become less confident, scared, and angry. This is what we have termed as "jealousy." The situation described above is a trigger to feeling jealous. The following are common situations that will help you identify triggers of jealousy.

*1. You worry that your partner's family or friends are encouraging your partner's undesirable behavior.*

There are situations where your partner has friends or family members who influence them to do things that can potentially end up causing tension in your relationship. It is something that you cannot ignore and hope to change with time. However, in some cases, you yourself may be the one making up issues that cause tension to your relationship rather than the family or friends of your partner. You need to be sure that you are not making up issues. Ask yourself whether you approve your partner's friends or family. Do you try to manipulate your partner into believing that their family or friends are a bad influence? In a situation wherein you do not like your partner's friends or family for no valid reason, you probably have a controlling or possessive behavior, and it is advisable that you deal with it. In a situation wherein you both agree that some of your partner's friends or family members are a bad influence, then it is important that the two of you talk about it.

## 2. *Your partner puts themselves in situations with intentions to test your ability to trust.*

There are numerous things that a person may do in this context, which include staying up late, going to a party, or hanging out with friends of the opposite gender. Also, your partner may be deliberately avoiding answering their phone when you are calling. Relationships are about becoming vulnerable, and trust can be a major trigger. It is a fact that without trust, one can feel extremely uneasy in a relationship. In a relationship, if you constantly feel worried, sad, or moody, then it qualifies as a trigger for jealousy. There are others who go to the point of crying their hearts out because their partners are out having fun without them. While your partner's actions and activities could be to test your faith in them, you fear that they might go too far. Also, you may fear that in the course of their trials, they may come across someone better than you are. Women and men tend to fall in love differently. Women tend to love with the help of oxytocin, which is the trust molecule. It will build as one learns how to trust someone, and the only way to fully trust someone is to be patient.

## 3. *You realize that your partner is lying about small things.*

It is one of the main triggers for jealousy, whereby upon realizing that your partner lied, you become angry and insecure. In certain cases, your partner may lie about having done something you do not like because telling the truth will make you angry. Lying is not good, but when there is the possibility that you will become angry, it becomes hard for them to tell the truth. The unfortunate thing with lying is that it tends to creates suspicion and distrust in the relationship. It is common to think that if your partner is lying about small things, then they will be lying about major things, such as about being committed or about who and where they hang out. If it becomes a trend, then subconsciously one will become doubtful of everything their partner tells them. It is true that a feeling of jealousy comes along whenever you see them with other people. This is because you will think that they are dating someone else.

**4. You worry when they go out without informing you and without you knowing what they are doing and who they are with.**

It is true that there are people who do not worry about their partners' whereabouts as long as they are all right. Not worrying is not an indication that you do not love your partner well enough. There are situations where your worries are directed to certain mindsets, such as thinking that your partner is going to cheat on you. Surprisingly, some will go to the extent of unexpectedly showing up in an unexpected place or snooping around. The danger in doing this is that it may slowly drive you into madness and cause tension in your relationship. It is important to note that prohibiting a person from doing things that they love will hurt them, create discomfort, and eventually lead to consequences that will ruin your relationship.

**5. You feel insecure because your partner is in contact with an ex or frequently talks about them.**

Betrayal is the most immediate feeling in such a situation. Exes are known to be triggers for fear and insecurity in most relationships, especially in a situation where you feel there is still exists a spark between your partner and the ex. Worrying about this will trigger abandonment, anxiety, and jealousy. In that situation, you feel that another person is taking away your partner's admiration or love, which belongs rightfully to you. There are situations where the feeling of betrayal is justified, but not all. Of course, the feeling of jealousy has to be triggered by something that happened that made you feel insecure or threatened. This is one of the most difficult triggers to deal with, and the best approach is to deal with the fear of being replaced, fear of loss, and insecurity.

## 6. *You always worry because your partner has a history of infidelity.*

Unfortunately, if at one time you caught your partner cheating, it is difficult to trust them again completely. There are people who are quick to forgive and forget, but there are those who keep the case of infidelity as a point of reference. They are quick to relate to the issue of unfaithfulness when a similar situation comes up even when it may not be true. You might have been cheated in your relationship, and although you have given your partner another chance, you might still suspect that your partner is not being honest with you. It is easy to suspect that they are on dating apps or talking to other people.

The fact that your partner was unfaithful in a certain way or cheated on you causes a major drawback to the relationship, and it is hard to trust again. It makes you sensitive to small issues and makes you vulnerable to being insecure even in new relationships. In that case, when you find your partner with a person of the opposite gender, the quickest thought that comes to the mind is that they have an affair. The existence of insecurity is a major issue, and jealousy always prevails unless one finds a way to move past the hurt.

## 7. *You worry that your partner will leave you for someone else.*

It is a fact that only a small percentage of people are completely happy and confident in themselves. It is common to find a person who feels that they are too short, too thin, and overweight. A lot of people feel that they do not have a sexy body figure, and some even doubt their sexual performance. At a young age, one of the major worries is whether you are able to satisfy your partner sexually. On such basis among others, people tend to worry that their partners will look for a person they will be more satisfied with—someone who is more beautiful, funnier, or richer. When you are jealous, you always assume the worst scenarios in the relationship. Truthfully, there will always be someone more interesting, more intelligent, more attractive, and richer out there.

Remember, if your partner wants to leave you, there is nothing you can do since it is their decision. However, it is paramount that you take care of your spirit, heart, mind, and body because jealousy is harmful to a person's well-being.

**8. You fear that the issues you encountered in past relationships may happen again in the current relationship.**

It is noted that most triggers are about the past and develops fears of the future among most people. Traumatic events in the past are hard to escape even when a person starts a new relationship. Psychologists affirm that if someone experienced something that was traumatic at the beginning of their relationship, it would keep on recurring. For instance, if you found out that the person you were dating was married and you did not know, it could come up over and over again being a major fear of the future. Truthfully, the past events and encounters play a vital role in shaping one's present and the future. If you can manage to stay in the present and be at peace at the moment, then it will be easy to escape and realize that these triggers of jealousy are irrelevant.

## 9. You start to worry or feel insecure that your partner may have an emotional withdrawal.

In the case where your partner stops doing things that he used to do for you (for instance, calling or texting all the time), you may find yourself worrying that your partner is not giving you enough attention. If they are no longer complimenting you on small things, such as being smartly dressed, it can trigger your thoughts that they are having someone else. Such thoughts of them telling those things to other people will cause sadness and, in other cases, anger. If it may happen that you find them with another person who may even be a family member, you will be quick to react negatively. You may find yourself distracted, crying, or even causing a drama even without having all the facts about the situation. The feeling of insecurity that may have developed at that time is directly tied to the element of jealousy. Communication in a relationship is important and plays a tremendous role in addressing most challenges and issues faced by couples. While you may think that your partner is having someone else because they are less available, it may turn out that their lack of emotional availability may be caused by other reasons.

## 10. You are disappointed because of unmet expectations.

In most cases, while in a relationship, you expect and want to be treated in a special way by your partner. You expect them to remember your birthday or anniversary or even know things you like, such as your favorite meal or color. Also, over the years, there are various holidays, such as New Year's, Christmas, and Thanksgiving, not forgetting others such as Women's Day. You may be expecting a surprise from your partner in any of the holidays or special occasions. Thus, if your partner does not give you gifts or surprises, you may become anxious, and you may think that your relationship is not moving forward. Negative thoughts (such as the thought that your partner is no longer finding you special or they want to end your relationship for someone else) are common in such cases. However, you may find that none of that is true. That is why it is important to talk about holidays plans or what you would like to do with your partner.

# Chapter 9: How to Mentally Step Back from Jealous Reactions

As noted, if you demonstrate insecurity, anger, and fear without facts to justify your feelings, then you are jealous. Up to this point, the book has identified that jealousy has negative impacts on a person's well-being, peace of mind, heart, and even health. It is because jealousy can lead to stress, anxiety, and consequently, depression, which may lead to serious repercussions. Also, in certain cases, one may not be aware that they are jealous or that the reason that they are feeling angry or anxious is jealousy. There are many indications that you are feeling jealous.

One indication is when you find yourself interrogating your partner, which may be risky if not properly carried out. Another indication is when you find yourself investigating your partner by checking information on emails, text messages, and social media to look for clues that your partner is cheating. Also, another indication is when you secretly follow your partner to social events, work, or health club—or in other words, you are stalking. Another indication is when you test your partner to know if they are still interested in you by asking whether you are attractive. When you find yourself looking for your partner's reassurance and trying to control them, it clearly shows that you are jealous.

Jealousy is something that originates from the mind, and it is only through training your mind to be positive that you will be able to step back from jealous reactions.

## Becoming Aware

The first step that one should take in dealing with jealousy as an emotional reaction is becoming aware. The aspect of awareness will let you know that the stories you are making up in your mind are untrue. It is the basis of having clarity of things and events occurring in your life, and it prevents you from reacting to things and scenarios that your mind imagines. As this analysis has uncovered, anger and jealousy are emotional reactions that drive a person into believing things that are not true.

The aspects of awareness will help you in changing the things you believe. Most importantly, it will shape you thinking, perception, and take on things, preventing you from imagining the worst on everything. It will drive you into changing what you believe and what you project in your mind that results in the destructive emotional reactions. It is noted that even in the cases where there is justification for a negative reaction, anger and jealousy are harmful and will lead to bad ways of handling and dealing with situations. It is true that this is not a simple act as it sounds, but through a strategic approach and with time, it can be done. It begins with addressing the beliefs that make you develop jealousy, which is more effective than controlling your emotions.

## Recovering Personal Power

The fact that you are prone to jealousy means that you have already given up your personal power. You may ask how you gave up such power. Complaining, not setting healthy boundaries, having unproductive thoughts, and giving up your values drove you into losing your personal power. A jealous person feels powerless because they cannot determine or know whether they are valued by their partners, friends, colleagues, or family. The loss of control, sense of threat, and stress greatly undermine your personal power. Judging yourself in a negative way, such as feeling that you are not good enough or having low self-esteem, equates to giving up your power.

Regaining your power plays a vital role in dealing with jealousy. You will regain your power by stopping to engage negative thoughts, such as telling yourself that you do not count. Entertaining worries makes a person vulnerable to bad things, jealousy being one of them. Worrying is not good for you because it takes away your power bit by bit to the point where you are completely powerless. Other points in regaining personal power are developing your core self, allowing personal growth, and trusting in the higher power or process.

**Shifting Your Point of View**

The implication in this is a failure to entertain the story occupying your cognizance. Jealousy will drive you into imagining the worst in every situation, which means that the first thoughts or story that your mind develops is negative. The action of stepping back, in this case, will mean not to entertain such thoughts or distract yourself from them and encourage positive thoughts.

Always flowing to the point of view that renders you into experiencing negative emotions limits your creativity. If your mind always develops a negative story, such as being left for someone else or your partner having an affair with the person they are talking with, it will make you a prisoner to negative emotions. A suitable way is to doubt that negative belief that has first closed your mind. Do not entertain it and allow a positive story to emerge.

For instance, a colleague has moved into a new house. Positive jealousy would be to take this as a challenge to work harder. Also, by changing your point of view, you will be able to put yourself in the other person's shoes. For instance, your partner may be withdrawing from you because you are increasingly becoming negative, annoying, and increasingly suspicious. Normally, if people feel that they are not trusted enough, they tend to move away; hence, it is important to change your point of view. It will always give you some moment to drive the jealousy feelings away.

## Knowing the Beliefs and Values within You That Trigger Emotional Reactions

Core beliefs are thoughts and assumptions that you hold about yourself, others, and the world around you. For instance, if you believe that opposite genders cannot have genuine friendships, you will always doubt your partners. Also, if you believe that you are not beautiful, interesting, or intelligent enough, then you will always react negatively on the basis of these fears. The core beliefs that people have are always deeply seated in a person's mind, and although unrecognized, they constantly affect our lives.

You may believe that the world is full of selfish people or other people are better in their jobs than you are. Having a set of negative core beliefs, especially about yourself, directly affects your confidence and self-esteem. If you lack the aspect of trust, it means that you will be suspicious of another person's intention. It is harmful to see the world and people in a negative way. It will affect the world and what you are willing to share and give.

If your core beliefs are positive or optimistic, then you will live your life in a realistic and somewhat flexible manner. Contrastingly, if your beliefs are degrading and negative, then you will create rules of living that are based on fear—restricted and limited. Your core beliefs set the basic assumptions about your identity and place in the world. The experiences that a person encounters in the course of life can shape your core beliefs. However, it does not mean that you cannot change them if they are negatively affecting your life.

Because core beliefs are deeply tied with your personality, the consequences could be far-reaching. They directly influence a person's core belief and how they interpret things around them. Thus, shaping your core beliefs will mean telling your mind what to think and how to interpret the lives around you.

## The Other Approach Is Developing Control over Your Attention

It means controlling what you pay attention to as a way of controlling your life. In this context, it is about training your mind on the things to focus on. If you focus on negative things, then you will always have negative emotions and vice versa. Your attention determines the experiences you have, which in turn determines how you live your life.

The idea is for you to control distractions, maximize focus, and find your flow. For instance, you are sitting with your girlfriend, having a good time, then a smartly dressed man passes by. You start thinking that your woman admires the man. It may not be the case, and paying attention to such thoughts will lead to ruining the good time that you are having with your partner.

Developing control will help you to know when your control is being stolen away and decide not to flow with such thoughts and focus on the current things. Allowing distractions will lead to negative emotions. You should be able to direct your attention according to your goals and priorities. Paying attention to what matters will mean that simple and negative thoughts will not dissuade you from trusting your partner.

## Talk about the Feeling of Jealousy

Experts recommend sharing things that are disturbing you with someone you trust. There are people who find it easy to deal with something or escape negative thoughts by talking about it with someone. Similarly, you can mentally step back from jealousy by talking about it with the right person and, in a healthy way, express to them what you feel. Kind friends can greatly help you from sinking deeper into sorrows or negative effects of jealousy.

The person or friend you trust or seek when your negative feelings are triggered is the correct individual to contact at these instances. However, it is important to make sure that the person you choose for this can support you to stay on track, a kind person who wishes the best for you. A friend will serve as a channel to let out the irrational feelings and thoughts rather than entertaining them in your mind. A good friend will truthfully inform you that your thoughts are exaggerated and irrational. In doing so, you will have relieved yourself those negative feelings and take reasonable actions. At some point, it is recommended that one seeks the assistance of a therapist. An expert in the therapeutic industry can assist you in making sense of the feelings you are experiencing and can show you the way to handle them.

## Train Your Mind to Be Competitive, Appreciative, Encouraging, and Acknowledging

Being competitive means being at your best. In simple terms, you will have to train your mind into feeling like yourself and embracing positive qualities that will help you to avoid negative thoughts and emotions and focus on achieving personal goals. It is important to feel inspired. Connect with other people. If you want to respect people around you, you will have to be considerate and mindful of your interactions.

Similarly, if you want to feel a consistent love of your partner, then you also have to show love in all your actions daily. Do not allow negative thoughts and ideas to tell you otherwise. It is easy to compare yourself with friends, co-workers, and your partner's exes. You do this because you think that it will make you feel better. Unfortunately, it will lead you to feel inadequate. It will drag your self-esteem down, which leads to jealousy.

To deal with self-doubt, you can continually acknowledge your partner or co-worker when they do something well. Unproductive criticism goes deeper into your thoughts, while positive criticism helps each other feel valued and confident.

# Chapter 10: Gentle Approaches of Acceptance

One of the common misconceptions about love and relationships is that people who are really in love have to equally feel jealous about each other. Most people believe that people in a relationship get jealous over stupid things and that it's okay. This misconception is so ingrained in society, and people attempt to justify jealousy at all levels. The truth is, jealousy is not a sign of love. There are several triggers of jealousy and various negative effects associated with jealousy as identified above. Jealousy in relationships is real, and jealousy is a huge burden for most couples. The first thing toward dealing with jealousy of a moderate level is accepting that jealousy is so much present in our society. We have all experienced its taste in one way or another. However, we can break the cycle of jealousy in a gentle manner, reclaim our self-control, and seize driving ourselves and our partners crazy.

## Jealousy Can Strike Anyone

No one is a special human that they do not experience some types of emotions. Whether it is time, mates, resources, or passion, jealousy is a common feeling that occurs in humans as they compete over something that they hold dear to and are threatened. Whether it is an actual threat or an imaginary threat, different people tend to experience jealousy at different times and levels and for different reasons.

Therefore, do not beat yourself up once you feel jealous. After all, you are an individual who seeks to maximize your welfare and survival. The problem comes when we do not take into account how these jealous feelings lead us into behaving.

We fail to understand that every emotion creates a force in us that determines not just the decisions we make on a daily basis but also the speed of the decision and the consequent action. Just as every feeling begins with an external stimulus that generates responsive hormones in the body, jealousy is triggered by various external factors that create feelings within us, which determine how we react. These triggers are in our surroundings, and no one is fully secure from them. Especially with the rise of the internet and communication technologies, there are more triggers for jealousy every new day.

Also, do not judge someone so harshly whenever you realize that they are jealous of you—not especially when this person is your romantic partner. Seek to understand their human nature and look for ways to help them get over these detrimental feelings. Be a listening partner. Understand that today it could be them but tomorrow it could be you in that situation.

When addressed well, mild jealousy is okay. As it turns out, jealousy does not have to be a relationship killer. It could even strengthen a relationship bond if well utilized. It is already established that every time you experience jealousy feelings, a part of your needs has not been fulfilled.

Jealousy for a couple could serve as a potential wakeup call for partners to look into deeper underlying issues. Coming clean on the feelings can get the relationship rooted on solid ground. All that matters is uncovering the feelings behind your jealousy, which comes out as a secondary emotion. It gives you a chance for mutual reassurance where you get to appreciate each other and level up your efforts in keeping the fire in the relationship burning. It also helps you uncover the hidden negativities within you that you could not have otherwise known. Proper addressing could show that either of you experiences some painful childhood or considers themselves inferior in many senses.

## Jealousy Should Not Be the Reason You Part with Your Partner

The chances are that if you part with a partner because of jealousy, this will be a pattern, and you will never stay in a relationship. The secret is to stop escaping from the feelings holding you back but to embrace them and address them as they are.

Jealousy is real, and it is a strong feeling that has the capability of lasting a lifetime and messing your relations every time. What you may lack to realize is that the success of a future relationship depends on your ability to employ the lessons you learned from the previous relationship. Strive to become a better person every time. This cannot happen if you keep carrying jealousy burdens.

While it is okay to experience mild jealousy, it is not okay in any way to let all these painful moments pass without exploring the actual cause of the jealousy. You have to find suitable ways to address these feelings with your partner. As explored above, if you are together for the right reasons, then you can always address such feelings with your partner.

## You Should Not Let Jealousy Control You: Why Not Control Your Imagination?

Now, the biggest mistake that we do is allowing jealousy to control how we react, behave, and relate with our partners. Jealousy is a feeling so intense, but it is made worse by creating crazy imaginations in our heads that deceive us into thinking that something is true while it is far from the truth.

If your partner is late, for instance, you begin to imagine that they were out there hooking up with a perceived rival. You become frightened and angry, and suddenly, you are so cold. Your outburst of anger makes you behave so weirdly toward them, and you can hardly hold a conversation. If only you took a turn from your imagination, you would have communicated constructively with your partner and got a hold of details that they may not even tell you once you act cold. Controlling your jealousy feelings should be taken as a rule of thumb, lest jealousy overpowers you and destroys you.

**You Can Make It: You Can Feel Jealous but Control It**

Explored above are various ways that can help you control your emotions. To control these feelings, you have to establish that you and your partner are on the same page (i.e., the same commitment level) and that you understand each other's differences. Then you have to understand your triggers of jealousy to learn how you can effectively control jealousy. Most often, jealousy results from betrayal in the past fear of abandonment, inferiority complex, and having a flawed perception of your relationship or the overall concept of dating and relationships.

Therefore, identifying these aspects can help you accept what cannot be changed and strive to become a better person by changing what you can. You will begin to use your imagination to feel better, and you will have an overall positive outlook of your relationship and yourself.

## How about You Stop Making Unreasonable Comparisons?

Comparison is one of the greatest enemies of a relationship. You compare yourself with your partner. You compare yourself with a perceived rival (third party). You compare yourself with people who seem to be doing better than you, more successful, and more attractive.

All these comparisons occupy your mind such that you argue your points by keying in how another person would have put it. One thing that people forget is that in whatever level or position they are, someone else will always be taking the lead and another person lagging behind them.

Understanding that we can never be equal is a critical component of stopping self-comparison with others. Can you imagine a society where everyone was equal with the same level of education, intelligence, wealth, and even riches? And most outrageously, a situation where everyone looked the same? Wouldn't it be boring? It definitely would. However, the problem we have is that we take life as a serious competition against other people, and this denies us a chance to be happy and to appreciate ourselves.

**Nothing Is Permanent**

It is possible that most of the things we feel jealous about are not permanent. The best thing you can do is to work on yourself. Do not allow your partner to be the biggest part of your life to the point that you fear that if you parted you would not find another person to match with.

Harboring these fears only interferes with your way of thinking and leads you into exploring more options of how you can keep your partner. This flaws your judgment, and you'll fail to establish whether the two of you are compatible as you go on since you are only focusing on how to keep them. However, being free and ready to embrace things as they come makes you look at situations from an objective point of view rather than being subjective to your feelings.

Fearing to lose someone will always affect how you feel about yourself. Thinking like you cannot survive without your partner is like limiting your capabilities. However, if you put in your mind that nothing is permanent, you will learn to understand when your jealousy is not helping you, or it can save you from a dangerous situation that you might be overlooking.

Most of the psychopaths and narcissists that lure people into relationships manage to get people attracted to them so easily. Unfortunately, if you have such a partner and you concentrate on your insecurities and inferiority and start to feel bad about yourself while looking for a way to make the relationship work, you might be overlooking a critical red flag in your partner. Therefore, realize that nothing is permanent, and you will be able to realize when your jealousy is harmful and when it is helpful for you.

## Do Not Hold Too Tight

No matter how much you love your partner or how much you feel that they love you, seek to lessen your leash on them. Give them their space to be them. They do not have to involve you in everything they do. They do not have to always hang out with you. You do not own them. They have only taken a deliberate decision to commit to you, and no matter how committed they are, everyone needs some space at times.

Do they want to hang out with their friends over a weekend? Trust that they will be okay. Let them be and trust that they are responsible. Remember, the more you try to "imprison" them, the more they will begin to look for opportunities to escape this possessiveness.

If they are attending the gym with some "attractive" people of their opposite gender, let them. You do not have to ask them to look for a separate gym where they are not in contact with these "attractive" people. In fact, they may not find them as attractive as you think they are. However, if you try to keep them off, it will get into their mind that there is something about these perceived rivals they should probably look closer to see. Typically, trying to hold too tight sets you up for a big disappointment.

# Chapter 11: Exercises for Making Yourself Better

**Compete Only against Yourself**

This life is your own responsibility. Life has no rehearsal. That someone else is doing better than you should not bother you. What should bother you is if you are doing better than yesterday. The most successful people believed in their ability to reach milestones through consistent efforts and not unfairly comparing themselves with others. Strive to see that you are making an improvement in your life, not for others to see but for yourself.

Some people believe that it is good to be competitive against other people. While this pushes you out of your comfort zone and drives your willingness to do anything to reach your goal, this is not a permanent solution, and it does not improve you toward your destined future since you are measuring success based on the value system of other people. Once the time comes that you cannot keep up with them, you begin to envy them, and you become uncontrollably jealous. Your desire to win will always be fueled by the fear to fail, and it will not be according to your value system.

**Develop the Mind of a Winner**

A winning attitude is a tough attitude that never allows any distractions or drawbacks to take them down. Did someone humiliate you that you do not look good enough? Did someone say you could never be successful in your fitness journey? Did that make you feel like you want to quit and lock yourself up in a corner to cry? You have the most flawed attitude toward life and its various tidings.

Also, a winning attitude will never get you feeling worthless or like you have someone else to help you run your life. Rather, this attitude shows you that you have to get up each day with renewed energy to handle everything that comes your way. It empowers your thinking and allows you to handle every situation from a calm and mature point of view.

Typically, the mind of a winner is defined by mental strength. Mental strength ensures that you have greater satisfaction in life because you accept the way you are while you strive to improve the condition of your life. You will understand your core values better, and you will be able to differentiate between what bothers you and what does not.

Also, remember that you are different in your own unique way. Instead of trying to fit in by copying other people's value system, you need to embrace your uniqueness and believe in your power to achieve. With a tough mind, you will be more confident in your decisions and actions, trusting that your priorities reflect your values and beliefs.

Most people feel disapproved by other people's comments about them because they have not realized the values that they stand for. Mental toughness also increases your resilience, and you are able to visualize yourself as a winner; hence, you never give up no matter what. Equip yourself with a tough mind such that you are able to conquer every battle for the mind that other people bring to you.

**Develop Daily Good Habits**

Still, the most successful people have daily habits that keep them occupied and focused on their journey. They barely have time to misjudge others and to overthink, and they have no room for unreasonable conflicts. They understand that in order to accommodate one negative feeling, thought, or action, they would have to give up a daily task that is so important for them. Therefore, these people have time to relax, time to work, and time for family and friends; and each of these moments count the most for them. They would rather hold a meaningful conversation with someone rather than judge them for something they realized that did not make them happy. Therefore, it is important that you work on having the daily schedule that will give you a sense of direction, and you will be able to handle anything that comes your way maturely.

You will be surprised to see how good habits can shape your life and make every day worth looking forward to. Also, it will allow you to give a deaf ear to all negativities because you are focused on achieving your daily schedule.

Start by creating a schedule that works for you. A schedule does not have to be fixed overnight. Try over time and see what works for you; then you can stick with it.

**Eat Healthy, Dress Smart, and Exercise**

One of the most encouraging things in someone's life is to know that they are smart. It feels good when you walk into an office and you command respect. You are confident that other people see your effort in taking care of yourself, and they actually admire that. Remember that self-confidence is a mental aspect, and aesthetically pleasant attire contributes to confidence.

Also, eating healthy is one of the important habits that most people know of but only a few practice it.

You should get it in your mind that your diet influences your energy levels and boosts your decision-making. It boosts your mood and helps to keep you generally happy.

Furthermore, exercising is the core of the functioning of your body. It is among the most important tools that nourish the mind and the body. It helps to keep you calm and reduce your stress levels, and the ultimate result is that you feel good about your body.

**Meditate**

Although meditation is becoming more common as people become more interested in living healthy lifestyles, most people have still not been able to implement the act of meditation in their lives. However, meditation is one of the simplest activities you can do. Try sparing some moment to close your eyes and pay attention to the rhythm of your breath. Try to pause your inhales and exhales for some seconds. Focus on the sensation of your breath as your muscles relax and the tension in your body declines.

Simple as it is, meditation can bring insurmountable benefits to your life, boosting your esteem and keeping you healthy. Meditation is an approved technique by scientists for combating anxiety, stress, and depression. It gives you the power to control your thoughts and allows you to calm the sound of any negative thoughts that may contribute to stress or low self-esteem in a constructive way.

Rather than trying to shut such feelings out (which would give them more power to control you), meditation allows you to look through them calmly, accept what cannot be changed, get ideas on how to improve what can be improved, and weaken these negative feelings in your system. It makes you realize that your feelings do not define who you are. Having thoughts that you are less worthwhile does not mean that you are incapable of achieving more. Meditation helps to categorically put these thoughts as they are and who you as a person are.

Essentially, realize that you have the power to control your thoughts and mind through meditation. It is about acknowledging that you can never control how others make you feel about yourself and make the negative thoughts have less power in you. Eventually, these feelings diminish, and you are more rejuvenated. You do not let any envious feelings bring you down, and you are more energetic to go about your day. Most importantly, you are able to hold meaningful conversations with your partner without your feelings getting in the way of this.

## Build Confidence

Confidence is a critical component for dealing with self-esteem issues. If you are not confident enough, then you are bound to face circumstances that turn you down and make you think of yourself as a failure. Building confidence begins with working on your mind. You have to cultivate within you a sense of achievement, although this should not turn you into a boastful individual.

Have you ever looked at someone who looks so good in doing something? Did you think about how flawless they were doing their thing? Now, that is confidence. The mistake that we commit most often is to think that these people were born with these capabilities. You would be surprised to find out how much effort they put into being good at what they were doing.

Confidence entails a state of mind with positive thinking and assurance in one's power and ability. Confidence gives you the ability to deal with stress, and it improves your emotional well-being. You have to visualize how you want to be and not have a poor perception of yourself. Calm your inner critic since this is the one thing that can make you see yourself as a failure. With this, you will be able to handle conversations with your partner in a mature way, and your negative self-image will not have to ask, directly or indirectly, for self-pity.

## Celebrate Small Successes

It might look trivial, but celebrating the little things in life is what drives us to an exponentially high level of achievement. While achieving big goals is a great source of joy for us, celebrating small victories in your daily life may just be what you need to stay motivated, stay away from negative feelings, and look forward to tomorrow. If you look closer, you will realize that you do things daily in your life that qualify as wins that go unnoticed. However, we are always quick to notice and give thoughts about our misdoings and mistakes. While it is important to notice our mistakes so that we can work on them, it is paramount that we acknowledge the small wins.

Acknowledging your wins is the core for your happiness and in relating with your partner. If you are able to appreciate your own wins, then you will also be quick to notice and acknowledge good things about your partner. You will highlight the good things always, and this will develop a way for you to table your feelings whenever there is a mishap.

Therefore, count your blessings. Do not concentrate on what you do not have. Also, concentrate on the good things about your partner. Get excited, live in the moment, and appreciate it. Do not pile unnecessary pressure upon yourself because this is what brings pressure and makes you unnecessarily jealous.

**Declutter Your Life**

Clutter is among the biggest burdens in our hearts and in our minds. It entails the various things we possess around us that we do not necessarily need. Learn to throw or give away the items that you do not use. Start by the simple cleaning exercises where you clear things in your kitchen or bedroom drawer that fill up your space. Eliminate everything from your desk that you do not need. We live in times when we possess too much. In our homes and in our lives, everything is just too much available for us. We possess mobile devices that store too much, much more than we require. Learn to eliminate these. Delete those applications in your phone that do not help you.

Furthermore, translate this cleaning exercise into your life. Get rid of all the negativity—whether it is a bad friendship, a social media account that feed you with a lot of negativity, pointless arguments, and even the goals that you are not able to hold together.

Take it as a general principle to always eliminate the 80 percent of the stuff that does not bring you success and happiness and focus on the 20 percent that is helpful for you. You will be able to free your mind and give it space to handle the most important things in your life. Your judgment about situations in your relationship will not be clouded, and you will have a better quality of relations with your partner.

# Chapter 12: Loving Yourself Unconditionally

Loving yourself unconditionally is the best gift you can give to yourself. Others might see you as a failure; you might be feeling like you have achieved only so little. In fact, you may not have achieved so much. However, so what? This is your journey, and no one can take it better than you. Learn to love yourself all the way and do not let anyone bring you down.

Furthermore, the first step into loving others is always to love you. Every reaction that you have toward others is determined by whatever is within you. The phrase "Love yourself" has become commonplace as the society increasingly throws at us issues that diminish our attitude of self-love. This idea of unconditional self-love is great but is so difficult to achieve for many.

In an era where other people's achievements are broadcast through the digital media and social media, there are myriads of ways to disrupt us from loving ourselves, with the greatest thief of our self-love being our perceived inadequacy and lack of achievement. Whenever you are feeling hopeless, irritable, or stressed, it is hard to love yourself as you should. Loving yourself does not come so naturally when life has given yourself 100 reasons to hate yourself, consider yourself as a failure, and question your thinking, beliefs, and values.

The following is a checklist of things you should know in order to love yourself even when it feels impossible:

**Approve of yourself:** True freedom comes in realizing that it is no one's job to approve of us or understand us. Rather, it is our own job to approve of us, appreciate us, and motivate us constantly. One of the major reasons why we are unable to love ourselves unconditionally is that we give other people too much power to have a say in our lives. We believe in their voices as the truth of who we are. We keep our hearts wide open for other people's judgment of us, yet we hold the greatest power to explore our deepest worth and stick on this. Therefore, realize that everyone has their own opinion of who you are but that it is your own opinion that counts. You are who you believe you are.

**Do not be too hard on yourself:** If you are too hard on yourself, you will always justify your personal criticism. You will always think like a perfectionist who tends to have no rooms for mistakes. You will even beat yourself up for the errors that have insignificant consequences on you. Even after correcting a mistake, you will always punish yourself. Also, you will always prioritize other tasks ahead of your self-care. Also, you will justify other people's actions when they treat you poorly because you think you deserved that treatment.

Therefore, do not be too hard on yourself. Learn to let your past mistakes go. You probably did not know the best techniques with which to handle things, you probably did the best you could, or you feel you could have done better. However, the past is in the past.

That is where it belongs, and this is where you are now. You have grown, you have learned more, and you can start living differently now. Forgiving yourself will teach you to forgive others also. You will be able to eliminate negativity and low self-esteem and have meaningful relationships with others.

**Love others and be kind to them:** Do not turn people down or downplay their efforts. Seize criticizing others because you will realize that they are doing better, and this will deny you happiness. Be kind to others because you do not understand their struggles. As the universe has it, your life is a reflection of what you give out. Give out love, and you will be able to appreciate and love yourself more.

**Do your mirror work:** It might look inconsequential, but looking at yourself in the mirror to get in contact with your own eyes allows you to appreciate yourself more than anyone else can. It opens the gate into your heart because it is at this moment you are able to appreciate your beauty and speak life into yourself.

**Nourish your mind with knowledge and wisdom:** Seek to equip yourself with knowledge and wisdom, and you will become unbeatable. Research on anything you want to understand. In the world today, learning materials have become so close to us through the internet. Instead of using the internet and social networking sites for just fun and filling your mind with things that only turn you down, use it for the benefit of yourself and become knowledgeable. You will understand more things, and you will become more confident in the person that you are.

**Daily affirmations:** "I am wonderful," "I am able," "I am blessed," "I can do it"—these phrases can do magic in your life and turn everything for your favor. If there is someone who talks to you more than any other person in the world, it is you. Why not take this chance to love yourself and improve yourself? Make sure that the words you tell yourself speak life to your soul.

Also, remember that the mouth speaks whatever is abundant in your heart. Therefore, ensure that your heart harbors positive thoughts even though the outside environment feels tough. Whatever you can speak, believe that you can achieve, and you will. The power of the tongue has it that whatever comes out of your mouth determines how things turn out in your life.

**Do something that you are good at often:** One of the things that discourage us most is the failure to achieve anything that we set out to do. Although it is good to challenge ourselves with big goals and achieve far much higher than our expectations, it is also good to balance such goals with doing things in which we are very good at.

Therefore, set achievable goals that will make you proud. Sometimes goals that are challenging get us exhausted, and there is no chance or willpower for self-love. Consequently, our burdens and exhaustion reflect on how we treat people we relate with frequently and mostly our partners. Also, it lowers our self-esteem, and we begin to envy people who have already achieved such big goals, forgetting that it took them a lot of time and consistent efforts to get there.

**Collect the good stuff:** Self-love is a result of consistent efforts to create a storehouse of positivity. If something is good and it makes you feel good, keep it. The essential meaning behind this is to have a place you can always go and find the symbols of the things that make you feel good. Be it a notebook, a personal box, or a folder in your computer, have a place where you can point out all the stuff that makes you proud in your life. These can be as minor as the smallest gifts you have received, certificates of merit, nice messages you have received, pieces of writing that you feel good about, or pictures that give you good memories.

**Surround yourself with positive energy:** Once you declutter your life as explained above, you should seek to establish strategic connections (such as a mentor), create more time for family and friends, and be with a partner who loves you for you. Such are the things that keep you motivated and lead you into exploring your higher potential. It is directly linked to feeling happy and valued. Being exposed to criticism and often looked down upon is not healthy for our souls, after all. Therefore, you should learn to surround yourself with people who love you for who you are.

Essentially, make sure you love yourself unconditionally and at all times. By loving yourself, you will become more confident, and you will not be prone to unnecessary triggers for jealousy, and you will be more powerful to overcome jealous emotions whenever they attack you.

# Chapter 13: How to Deal with Another Person's Jealousy toward You

It feels bad when you realize that your partner, friends, or people around are jealous toward you. The aspect of a partner being jealous toward you mostly comes as a result of being insecure with the things you are doing. In the case of co-workers, friends, or families, they tend to be jealous when you succeed in a given endeavor. When you succeed in something, it is unfortunate that not all people around you will feel proud or positive about that success. A feeling of jealousy can cause uncomfortable situations, and in some cases, you may feel bad about your success. It is an unpleasant feeling when other people are jealous of you, especially friends and family. Positive jealousy is good because it motivates and inspires those who experience it to change their lives positively and make progress like you have made. However, for negative jealousy, it is a whole different story and will make you experience unpleasant emotion.

In the case of a romantic relationship, dealing with a partner who is jealous requires effective communication. Unlike other people, your partner is an easy person to approach and engage in a conversation about their negative emotions or rather the insecurities they have in the relationship. The first course of action is to inform them how you feel. It is important to use the "I" statements—for instance, "I feel uncomfortable when you change your moods when you see me with a female friend."

Explaining the situation and pointing out exactly what you feel about certain things (especially actual things that they do) lay the basis for an effective and productive discussion. In so doing, you are describing the behavior that is upsetting you. It is more of pointing out the behaviors you observe about them rather than continuing to assume that things will automatically be all right.

When you are dealing with the issue of romantic jealousy, how you approach the things you are discussing will determine its success. It is advisable to avoid giving ultimatums, making assumptions, mind-reading, moralizing, threatening, overgeneralizing, or using labels. Talking about the behavior as a specific action will more likely make the person feel less guilty and resentful compared to when you confront them with assuming statements that people mostly use.

Furthermore, it is important to explain how their action effects. Communication will be effective if you can explain why you feel the way that you do. For instance, reflect on your expectations, anticipations, feelings, memories, and understandings in the relationship in relation to jealous behavior. For instance, you can tell them, "I feel anxious when you ask me if I meet with my exes because it shows that you do not trust me." However, you should avoid blaming your feelings on your partner in the explanation that you provide.

There are areas where romantic jealousy is similar to other forms of jealousy. The suitable basis with this sort of jealousy is to understand the signs. It is hard to deal and associate with people who you know feel jealous toward you. Although you cannot control other people's emotions, recognizing the signs can help you to fix it.

**One sign is false praise:** Mostly, a person who is jealous about you will be the first one to give a compliment that sounds sincere, but unfortunately, these people will be rolling eyes when you leave their sight. In most cases, such people find it easy to pretend that they are not jealous rather than deal with the issue. The advisable way to do this is to give them a sincere compliment whenever something positive and good happens in their lives. The essence in doing this is to show that you are an honest and genuine person and you mean good toward them. In turn, it will help curb their jealousy.

**The other sign is that a person downplays your success:** You may have a person in your life who, no matter what you achieve, will make it appear like it was by chance. You may have worked very hard for what you have achieved, but that person tells you that you did not work as hard to achieve success. It is a person who always gives you condescending or rude reasons for various things. It does not mean that such a person is not a close friend. The person could be your colleague or a close friend whom you always relate. You may be forced to hide your success to that friend to avoid their negative comments and criticism. You should not take the bait and try to prove that you worked hard or you deserved the success that you made. The suitable way to deal with the issue is to stay humble but remain firm in your achievements. You should not brag or try to prove yourself or even try to point out more success that you will achieve in the future because in doing so, you are more likely to make them stay jealous of you.

**If someone who is flaunting about their success to you, it is a sign of jealousy:** You may have a friend who is always talking about their success in an extensive way or trying to magnify what they have achieved. A person who is jealous about the progress you are making in life will be more inclined to flaunt their achievements when you have celebrated your own success. Truthfully, a person will flaunt about their success in the first place because they are not successful in the same way as you are. These are people who are always filled with negative thoughts to the people who envy them and about themselves for having failed to achieve their goals. As a way of dealing with this, getting upset about this issue will make them feel more justified about flaunting. The suitable way to handle such a situation is to offer them sincere praise about their achievement. In pointing out sincere praise, you will make the person stop feeling negative toward you and them.

**Sadly, another sign that a person is jealous of you is if they are imitating you:** It is more of a person who competes with you. There is a positive competition if a person will not hide their admiration and will openly term you as their role model. However, there are those whom you feel and experience tension and awkwardness when with them because their efforts to compete are not honest. These are people who want to be just like you or want to be better than you. One simple indicator of such a person is that they may dress or talk like you in order to feel better about themselves. You may fail to adequately deal with this situation if you react with anger or you become upset. The advisable way to handle this situation is to encourage them to go their own way. When you see that they are doing their own thing, you may give reliable advice. You should advise them that they do not have to imitate you to be great, but they can be their own person.

**A person who celebrates your failures is jealous of you:** There is only one reason why someone will find pleasure or derive happiness from your failure in the course of your life. That person is jealous and fears that your success will make you outstanding. Also, in celebrating your failure, such a person is afraid that you will succeed more than they have. There are people who go as far as strategizing how you will fail. For instance, a person reports untruthful things to your supervisor upon learning that you may be promoted. Also, a person may go as far as telling your potential partner negative things about you to destroy the relationship. There are others who celebrate secretly and enjoy your failures. The best way to handle such people is by taking your mistakes with grace and owning your failures. Strong people do not give up when they fail and work hard to achieve more. You can remind those who celebrate your failures by words and actions that making mistakes is part of learning and life. If they realize that you are not upset or you do not give up about the failures, they will be dissuaded because they will not be getting the enjoyment that they hoped they would.

**A person who gossips behind your back:** This is a common sign of a person who is jealous of you. They find it suitable to tell made-up stories about you to anyone who wants to listen to them. Most people who gossip do not talk about positive things; instead, you will find them making things up. The things that they say about you may be hurting and malicious in a way, and when you hear them, you will be disappointed. For instance, you may buy a new car, and someone gossips that you stole the money or you have a rich sexual partner who is financing your life. Similarly, in the workplace, when you move to a new home, someone may say that you have embezzled company funds or lured clients. There are numerous negative things that a person can say about you. The most appropriate way to deal with a person with that sort of jealousy toward you is to confront them directly. You should not make a mistake of gossiping back about that person because, in doing so, you will have created a series of events that may never end, or it may worsen the situation to the point of becoming physical with them. If you talk to them on a serious tone about what they are doing, they may rethink their behavior, and it may stop it completely.

**Competitiveness is also a sign of jealous:** As identified, there is positive competition and negative competition. Positive competition is based on a genuine basis of willing to perform well and improve your well-being, among other achievements. Unfortunately, negative competition is equivalent to jealousy because it is based on bad emotions. Jealous people tend to be highly competitive because they want to be the one succeeding or having the good things that they think that you have. These are people who wish that they are the ones who got the job that you have, the car you just bought, the house you moved to, or the fiancé that you have.

Jealous people are either arrogant or insecure, and all they want is to prove superiority. Sometimes it is tempting to compete with them, and most people fail to handle this situation favorable by making the competition unhealthy. In doing so, you will make the person more vigorous and make them hate you more.

Having haters may not appear as an issue, but it is advisable to avoid this sort of energy. Thus, what you should do is to refuse to play this game by acting naturally and doing your things in the usual manners. This will lower their interest to compete.

If you have a friend who keeps saying that situations are unfair because you have certain things and they do not have, it is a sign of jealousy: This is common. Perhaps you have a friend who always says that it is unfair that you have a job and they do not, that you have a fiancée and they don't, or that you are making a large amount of money and they are not. As noted, it may relate to numerous things, but that person expresses sadness because their life has not turned out to be good as yours have turned out to be. It is like the person is feeling bad because you have achieved something that they have not. If that person does not express their feelings in a positive way, it means they are jealous. Most of the time, they secretly wish that you do not achieve anything in life so that you do not leave them far behind.

People tend to blame outside forces and circumstances for what you have achieved that they have not. The best way to handle that person is not to put them down but try to encourage them in what they are doing in life. You can encourage them and help them to find a job. If they are already working, you can advise them on how to save. The positive message, in this case, will drive the person into becoming more positive in life.

**Also, in most cases, a person who hates you is jealous of you:** In your life, you may have people who were once friends but later developed hatred toward you for no reason. Also, it may be a colleague who hates you for no conceivable reason. Truthfully, they may just be jealous, but it is not because you wronged them in any way. You can agree that this is a challenging situation to deal with because a person who hates you will avoid any sort of interaction with you as much as possible.

In most cases, people tend to separate themselves from such people and treat them in the same way that they treat you. Any sort of interaction with that person will occur when it is not avoidable or demanding. In certain case, you may feel the urge to show this person that you are likable or a genuine person. If it is not possible to make that person like you, then you can just cut that person from your life. It is not healthy to have such negativity, especially if they just hate you for no reason. Thus, the best solution to this case is to let go.

# Chapter 14: Real-Life Examples of Jealousy Cases and Solutions

There are many references to jealousy as it has existed since the beginning of times. For instance, in the biblical story, the fraternal relationship between Abel and Cain broke because of the jealousy of one party. Also, the popular Trojan War in Greek was sparked by jealousy.

There are several examples of jealousy cases in relationships in society today.

**A Case of Jealousy after Betrayal**

If you have suffered betrayal in the past, you might be envious of something as simple as your partner receiving a text message from their ex-lover or simply admiring another person. You might want to follow each of their steps, but what this does for you is only to drive them further from you and to hurt your feelings. Therefore, the best solution you can employ is to work on healing, let go of your past, control your emotions through the methods discussed above, and constantly communicate with your partner in a constructive manner.

## A Case of Inferiority Complex

If you have low self-esteem and someone out there gives you a mean comment, you might think that your partner also notices the "weakness" pointed out by the person out there. This might go to your head, and you might end up thinking that your partner will eventually leave you. You will go down the road of self-pity, and you will be jealous over imaginary rivals. You cannot communicate to your partner well, and you cannot handle seeing them talk to other people that you think are a potential threat to your relationship. Instead of carrying this burden, learn how to love yourself unconditionally, improve in the areas that you can improve, and accept the things that you cannot change. This will give you an easy time relating to your partner.

## A Case of Assumptions

Assumptions in a relationship cause trouble because they get you jealous over unnecessary cases. Instead of clarifying when a situation doesn't seem to add up, you end up judging your partner over it, and this becomes disastrous. For instance, if your partner did not buy you a meal and they are full when they got home so they did not have to eat, you might become furious, assuming that they deliberately did not get you a meal. You confront them angrily, and this creates tension between the both of you. You are furious, and you also hurt their feelings because they mean the best for you but you accused them of being selfish. Instead of creating such a scenario, keep it in your mind that your partner has your best interest at heart. Walk away, calm down, and ask them later about it. You will be surprised that it has genuinely not crossed their mind that you would need a meal at that time. Learn to communicate with your partner constantly. Rather than assuming they know you want something, ask them to get you that thing.

## A Case of Expectations

Expectations breed jealousy because everyone has different expectations. You and your partner cannot be similar in every feeling and in every thought. Led by your wild expectations, you might get jealous when your partner talks to other people whom you perceive to be rivals. This is led by the thought that they are supposed to stick with you and not talk to others. Rather than addressing this issue effectively, you get overwhelmed, and you begin to fear to lose them, which hurts you and influences your behavior toward them. To avoid holding such an expectation, make sure you explore your views and your partner's views on how a healthy relationship should be maintained. Also, ensure to get things clear from the beginning. Seek to know exactly what both of you are up to in the relationship and your level of commitment. Most importantly, learn to not expect too much from your partner. No one can really complete you more than you. Love yourself first and keep open and constructive communication with your partner.

## A Case of Investment in the Relationship

In the event that you have invested so much into the relationship and your partner does not replicate your efforts, you might get jealous. For instance, if you are a man and you invest a lot of money and time on your partner (a lady) and they fail to love you right back, you might get jealous and start wondering whether she is seeing other people. You begin to think that maybe she wants to be with someone else and not you, who have invested a lot in pleasing her. You become furious, and feelings of disappointment, fear, and insecurities reflect on how you behave toward her.

Instead of creating such an ugly situation, seek to understand your partner's intentions from the beginning. Seek to establish a connection and a solid framework for your relationship rather than investing blindly in pleasing your partner. Also, realize that the exact result that you hope for when you are investing does not have to happen. There are variances to this, and you should learn to accept results as they are. Just like a gambler, know when to quit and when to hold on.

## A Case of Aging

When you find that your partner is talking to someone younger than you, someone who looks more appealing physically and more successful, you might become jealous, and this might lower your self-esteem. You might find yourself trying to unfairly guard your partner away from them, become possessive and becoming unnecessarily bitter toward your partner.

To avoid this situation, embrace yourself, learn to love yourself unconditionally, and talk to your partner. These perceived rivals might not be pleasing your partner as you think they are. Constantly communicate with your partner to ensure that you are on the same page and that nothing has changed in their goals and intentions with you. Also, realize that you can begin right now. You can live an amazing life for the rest of it. Stop envying someone for something you cannot regain. Age, once lost, cannot be recovered.

# Chapter 15: Recap: Summary of Lessons Learned and How to Maintain a Healthy Relationship

Up to this point, the book shows that jealousy is a common issue in your relationships with friends or family members and at work. Unfortunately, jealousy is attributed by negative emotions such as anger, insecurity, and powerlessness—all that in different ways make life hard. Jealousy affects a person's well-being, ability to be in a good mood, and relationship with other people.

Also, we have identified that jealousy will affect your quality of life in numerous ways. Jealousy can be positive or negative, and the latter is harmful to a person's well-being, growth, and social life.

Positive jealousy in a relationship is the type of jealousy that does not control you; rather, you control and drive it. It helps you uncover things that can help improve your relationship, and it helps you discover issues that would not have been discovered otherwise.

For instance, you found out that your partner is flirting with another woman, so you talk about it with your partner and realize what is lacking in your relationship. In the context of friends, co-workers, or family, an example of positive jealousy is when, upon seeing something they own that you also want to have (e.g., new furniture or new mansion), you are motivated to work harder to achieve the same or better. You do not hate or get angry with them nor feel insecure because they have made such improvement in their lives.

You should note that negative jealousy is bad to you, your partner, friends or family, or the person you are jealousy with because it destroys your relationship. This form of jealousy is founded on bad grounds, mostly by failing to trust and being insecure.

Truthfully, by being jealous, you drive people away because it is one of the negative forces that people not only hate but also fear. You may have heard cases where lovers kill each other, and nowadays, these cases are numerous, especially among young people.

People are becoming conscious and scared of jealous lovers or partners, and upon learning that you a jealous type of person, they may have to leave the relationship even if they love you. Jealousy is a condition where you feel insecure and you do not trust that you are enough for your partner. It has been discussed extensively in simple terms that if your partner having friends with the opposite gender does not mean that they are cheating. Also, if a person close to you is doing better than you in life, it does not mean that life is unfair. Take things easy. Listen, learn, and most importantly, do not let jealousy ruin you.

This book has provided you proper guidance on how you can identify your jealousy triggers and how you can deal with them. Most of the time, jealousy is triggered by how you think of your partner and the people around them. Jealousy is about worrying, being insecure, or getting agitated when your partner hangs out with family or friends that you consider being a bad influence.

If you worry that your partner is lying to you and that they are engaging in suspicious activities, it may be because you are jealous. In another case, you may find yourself worrying because your partner goes to places or events without informing you. As we have discussed, there are numerous thoughts that may be going on your mind. You might think they are finding it satisfying to take someone else with them instead of you. However, you may be surprised to find that your partner is not going with anyone or they avoid telling you because they know you will get upset.

The triggers that you experience about jealousy occur from your brain. It is the brain that triggers your emotions. As we have seen, jealousy originates from lacking faith or trust in other people. In certain cases, jealousy may be triggered by some past events. You might have been cheated in your previous relationship, or something bad might have happened to you.

In some re cases, you are worried because your partner is in contact with their exes. It is a major trigger, and truthfully, everyone will be suspicious and insecure of such contact, knowing that those people were intimate at one time. You feel that they might get back to each other. Of course, it is worse if your partner has a history of infidelity or at one time you caught them cheating or flirting with another person. The bad thing with this is that you will be growing suspicious every moment. These events lead to the fear of being left for someone else. There is no worse fear in a relationship than being left for someone else, and a key trigger to this is jealousy.

A key lesson is how you can deal with jealousy now that you have realized why you experience this sort of emotion. It is true that emotions are not easy to deal with, and you cannot just ignore them nor shut them. However, if you can train your mind to think differently, take things differently, and develop a different point of view or perception besides the one that drives you into feeling jealous, it would be easy to overcome it.

As we have identified, the key reason why people become jealous is that they do not believe in themselves. They have low self-esteem. They do not accept their strengths or weaknesses, so they give up their power over their own thoughts. If you take back this power, you take back your self-esteem.

Never think that you are not good enough. You may have heard a person saying that they know they are the best thing that happened in their partner's life. A person will be confident enough not only to say that but also to believe it if they have their personal power intact. Refrain from giving up your power. Be open-minded. Do not think that you are not good enough or not attractive enough, among other problems. Start with loving yourself. When you have self-love, that's when you start to believe that other people will love you for who you are.

More importantly, you may not be the one who is jealous. Your partner or someone close to you may be the one jealous of you. You may agree with the analysis concluded in this book that when someone is jealous of you, it affects your relationship.

There exists a tension, and somehow, you are not sure how to handle it or how to react. When it comes to your partner, we have found that the best way to deal with it is to have open communication. An open, honest dialogue with your partner will save your relationship with many troubles. Begin by telling them how you feel and what their attitude and behavior are doing to your relationship, and get their side of the story.

In other cases, the person who is jealous of you may be a colleague, co-worker, friend, or family. While in most cases, you may lack a good platform to engage a conversation about what you feel, it is important to talk with them. You may notice that they are jealous of you as a result of many things. You can easily spot these people—they are those who see you as a competitor, those who try to imitate you, those who hate you, or those who over-congratulate you.

The best approach to deal with such people is to be positive and humble. It will not help to be rude or to give in to the jealous person's games. It will only mean that the trend of jealousy will continue.

# Conclusion

We have discussed and pointed out numerous things that are related to jealousy. Jealousy is a negative emotion that, when not correctly dealt with, could lead to serious mental conditions, such as stress, anxiety, and depression. The most direct implication of being jealous is that you tend to be angry, anxious, insecure, fearful, and unsure of yourself. It is one of the worst feelings, and the bad thing about it is that it can ruin relationships.

Jealousy is a negative emotion, and it is best to handle it properly. Not surprisingly, jealousy will lower your quality of life and the way you relate with other people.

In some cases, you may feel that it is justifiable to be jealous—for instance, if you have been lied to or cheated in the past or if you have experienced any other thing that is unfavorable. In most cases, these justifications are not on a credible ground. You may find that the fears or thoughts that you have are generally unfounded. Take, for instance, the issue of trust. If your partner realizes that you don't trust them, for a short period of time, they will try to prove to you that you can trust them. If they realize that there is no improvement, most of the time, they will opt to discontinue the relationship. You may later regret upon realizing that you were jealous for no reason.

However, this does not mean that there are no cases of genuine or justifiable jealousy. It is found that there is no point in stressing yourself if you have no facts about the case or the issue. For example, you might be worried that your partner will leave for someone else. Truthfully, your being jealous will not help you, and neither will it help your partner. It may worsen the situation by making your partner discontent and making them develop negative emotions toward you.

There is no point in torturing yourself or subjecting yourself to such a hideous situation. The truth is, if someone wants to leave you, there is nothing you can do to stop them. Jealousy will just hurt your feelings. It is helpful to be objective about things, and more importantly, always have confidence in yourself.

The ability to feel the best version of you at all times is achieved if you are not worried that there is someone more beautiful than you, funnier than you, or more intelligent than you. There will always be people out there that are better than you in many things, but always remember that there are also good things about you that your partner loves, and that is why they are with you. In believing so, you will be able to overcome jealousy.

Finally, it is important to know that, sometimes, it all has to do with your core beliefs. For instance, if you believe that a male and a female cannot work without having an affair, then you will always be anxious whenever your partner is with someone of the opposite gender.

You should know that not everyone shares the same belief system as you. In certain instances, it is helpful to question your belief system and identify whether it is misguiding you. Always remember that making a decision when you are emotional will always lead to regrets. We have identified that dealing with your jealousy is a challenging task, but if you train your brain not to take the simple line of thoughts that involves imagining the worst in a given scenario, it will be helpful.

# Bibliography

Batey, H., May, J., and Andrade, J. (2010). Negative intrusive thoughts and dissociation as risk factors for self-harm. Suicide and Life-Threatening Behavior, 40(1), 35–49.

Ellis, C., and Weinstein, E. (1986). Jealousy and the social psychology of emotional experience. Journal of Social and Personal Relationships, 3(3), 337–357.

Kristjánsson, K. (2016). A philosophical critique of psychological studies of emotion: the example of jealousy. Philosophical Explorations, 19(3), 238–251.

Printed in Great Britain
by Amazon